# SOUNDS

## Selected Topics

**J J Wellington** BSc MA

**Stanley Thornes (Publishers) Ltd**

Extending Science Series

| | | |
|---|---|---|
| 1 | Air | E N Ramsden and R E Lee |
| 2 | Water | E N Ramsden and R E Lee |
| 3 | Diseases and Disorders | P T Bunyan |
| 4 | Sounds | J J Wellington |

Further titles are being planned, and the publishers would be grateful for suggestions from teachers.

---



First published 1984 by
Stanley Thornes (Publishers) Ltd
Educa House
Old Station Drive
Leckhampton
CHELTENHAM GL53 0DN

*An exception is made for the word puzzles on pp. 57 and 58. Teachers may photocopy a puzzle to save time for a pupil who would otherwise need to copy from his/her copy of the book. Teachers wishing to make multiple copies of a word puzzle for distribution to a class without individual copies of the book must apply to the publishers in the normal way.

British Library Cataloguing in Publication Data
Wellington, J.J.
Sound.—(Extending science; no. 4)
1. Sound—Juvenile literature
I. Title II. Series
534 QC225-5

ISBN 0-85950-134-5

Typeset by Tech-Set, Gateshead, Tyne & Wear.
Printed by Bell & Bain Ltd, Thornliebank, Glasgow.

# CONTENTS

## Chapter 1 **Introducing Sounds**



## Chapter 2 **Travelling Sounds**



## Chapter 3 **Hearing Sounds**



## Chapter 4 **Speaking**

## Chapter 5 **What a Racket!**



## Chapter 6 **The Sounds of Music**



## Chapter 7 **'Seeing' with Sounds**

# PREFACE

Everywhere you go you can hear sounds. They may be loud or quiet, high- or low-pitched, nice or nasty.

Sounds can be annoying. Sounds can be useful. Sounds can be musical.

This book tells you:

- how sounds are made
- how sounds travel
- which materials carry sounds
- how you hear sounds
- why some people cannot hear sounds
- how your voice makes sounds
- how sounds become noises
- how high- and low-pitched sounds are made
- how sounds become music
- why some sounds cannot be heard
- how sounds can be useful.

J J Wellington

# ACKNOWLEDGEMENTS

The author and publishers are grateful to the following who provided photographs and extracts and gave permission for reproduction:

Philip Clarke (p. 31); Clive Friend FIIP, Woodmansterne Ltd (p. 10); *Guinness Book of Records* (p. 33); Macmillan Publishers Ltd (p. 15); *The Observer* (p. 41); The Press Association (p. 33); Royal National Institute for the Deaf (p. 19); Royal Society for the Prevention of Accidents (p. 37).

The two crosswords were supplied by Mr D F Manley of ST(P).

# INTRODUCING SOUNDS

## DIFFERENT SOUNDS

Just close your eyes for twenty seconds. How many different sounds can you hear?

All around you there are sounds. Silence may be golden, but it is also very uncommon. Can you think of a place and a time where there would be no sound at all — complete silence?

Because there are so many different sounds around, there are many different words to describe them. Some of these words even sound like the sound itself and give you a sensation of it. Some examples are shown on the next page.

ACTIVITY 1

### Animal noises

Many animal noises have special words to describe them: the *purr* of a cat, the *howl* of a wolf, the *quack* of a duck. Make a list of all the animals and their word noises that *you* can think of. How well do you think the words *match* the sounds?

## WHERE DO SOUNDS COME FROM?

There are hundreds of different sounds, but they all have *one* thing in common. All sounds are made because something *moves.* Without movement there can be no sound.

Machines and engines make sounds when they are working, because their moving parts bang against each other. If you bang a drum, you can feel the drumskin moving. Twang a guitar string and touch it lightly with your finger. The string is moving. If you place your fingers gently on the front of your neck you will feel your voice box in your throat. Say *'Eeh . . .'.* Can you feel it moving?

*All objects making sounds are moving. A still object is a silent object.*

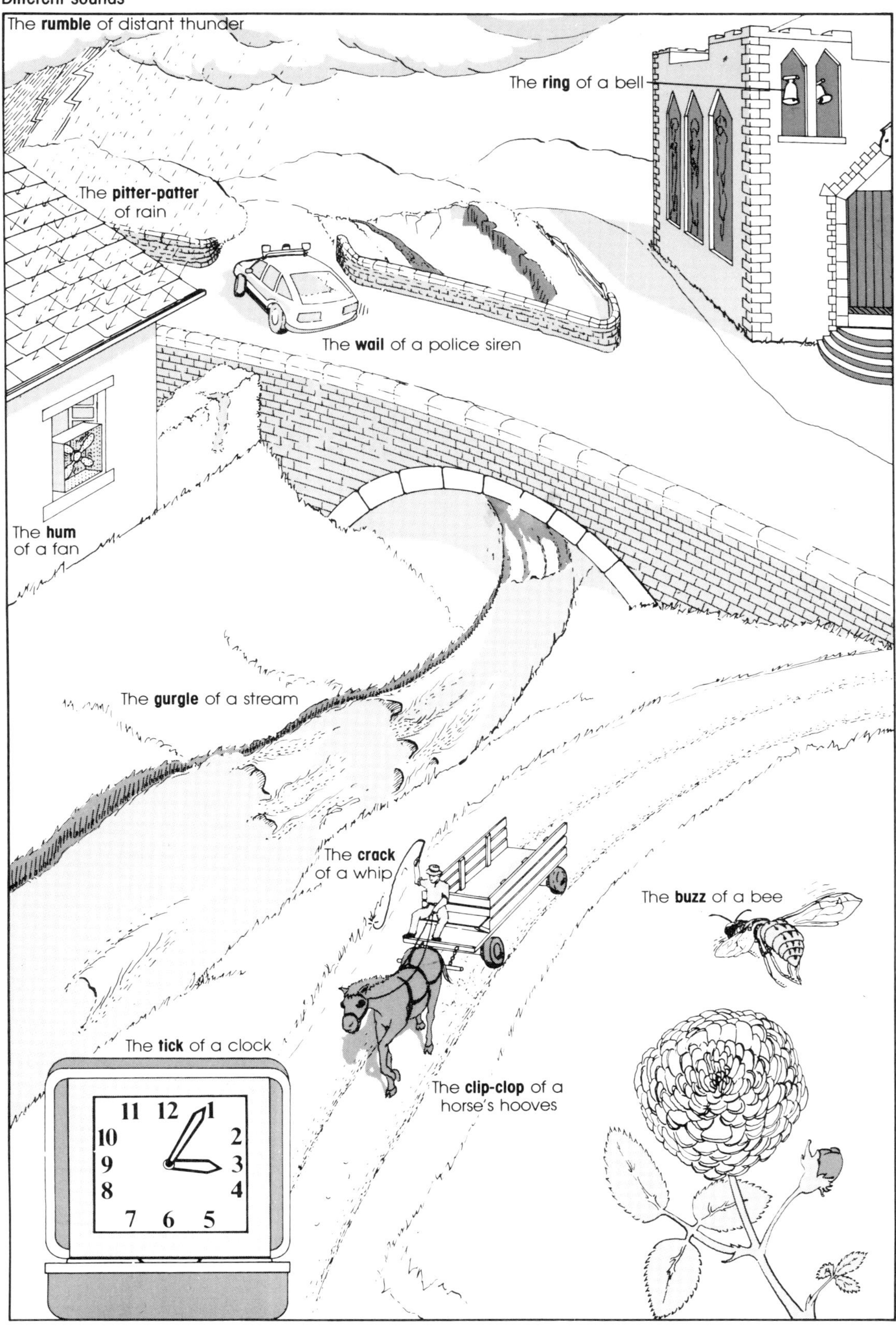
The **rumble** of distant thunder
The **ring** of a bell
The **pitter-patter** of rain
The **wail** of a police siren
The **hum** of a fan
The **gurgle** of a stream
The **crack** of a whip
The **buzz** of a bee
The **tick** of a clock
The **clip-clop** of a horse's hooves
11 12 1
10 2
9 3
8 4
7 6 5

ACTIVITY 2

### Making sounds

List as many different ways as you can of making sounds. What do these ways have in common? How are *all* sounds made?

## WHAT SORT OF MOVEMENTS MAKE SOUNDS?

Sounds are made by backwards-and-forwards or to-and-fro movements. These movements are examples of *vibrations.* When you twang a guitar string it vibrates. A moving drumskin is vibrating. There are special strings or 'chords' in your throat that vibrate when you speak or squeak. If you stretch an elastic band and pluck it, the band makes a 'twang'. It is vibrating. All sounds are made by something vibrating. These vibrations make the air around them vibrate too. This is how sounds are usually carried to your ears (as Chapter 2 explains).

## FAST AND SLOW VIBRATIONS

Whenever you hear a sound there *must* be something vibrating. The vibrations may be fast or they may be slow. The faster the vibration, the higher the *pitch* of the sound it makes. A thin guitar string vibrates more quickly than a thick string of the same length. The thin string makes a high note. The thick string gives a low note. High notes are said to be 'high-pitched' and low notes are 'low-pitched'. The pitch of different sounds and the way sounds can be put together to make music are described in Chapter 6.

Many vibrations are too fast for you to see. Some vibrations are so fast that the sounds they produce are too high-pitched for you to hear. (The study of these sounds is *ultrasonics,* the subject of Chapter 7.) Other vibrations may be so *slow* that they make no sound at all. Can you think of any examples?

ACTIVITY 3

### Experiments with vibrations

*Experiment 1*

Fix a piece of cardboard or plastic so that it touches the spokes of a bicycle wheel. Then ride the bicycle. As the wheel moves, what happens? As the wheel speeds up how does the sound change?

*Experiment 2*

Place a ruler with about a quarter of it over the edge of a table. Hold one end firmly. Pull down the other end and let it go. Listen to the sound. Now make more of the ruler jut out over the edge. Twang the ruler again. What has happened to the pitch? Lastly, hold the ruler firmly with almost *all* of it over the edge. Twang the free end, then gradually pull it back across the table. What do you hear?

Twanging a ruler

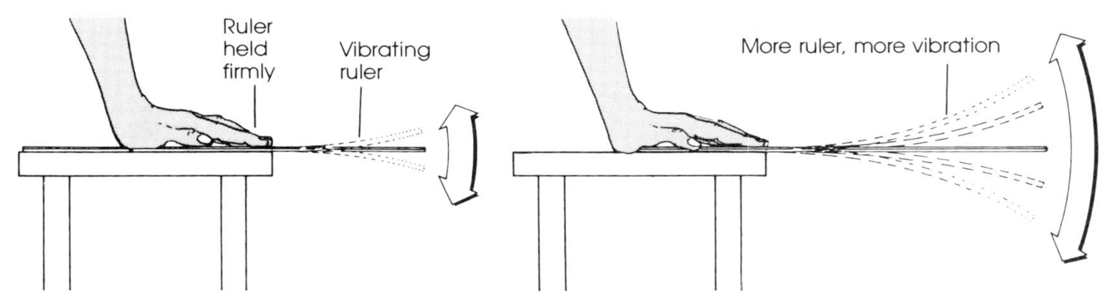


## STRONG AND WEAK VIBRATIONS

Some vibrations are much bigger and stronger than others. If you bang a drum hard, it vibrates strongly. The drum makes a *loud* sound. If you tap the same drum gently, it vibrates more weakly. The vibrations are smaller, and it makes a softer sound. Usually, the *larger* the vibrations the *louder* the sound.

| *Vibrations* that are . . . | strong | weak | fast | slow |
|---|---|---|---|---|
| make | | | | |
| *sounds* that are . . . | loud | soft | high-pitched | low-pitched |

**ACTIVITY 4**

### Tube and candle experiment

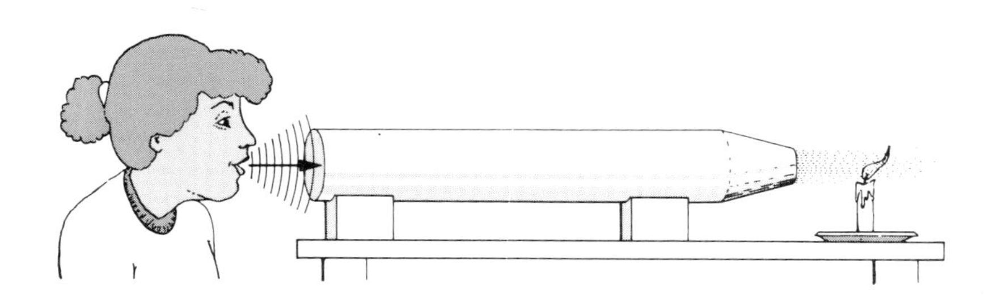

The tube and candle experiment

Strong vibrations and sounds often carry a lot of energy. If you whisper gently at one end of a tube, you can make a candle start to flicker. What do you think happens if you shout loudly down the tube?

Now try the same experiment with a radio at one end. Gradually turn the volume up. The vibrations become stronger — the sounds carry more energy.

Some sounds carry enough energy to damage your ears, as Chapters 3 and 5 explain.

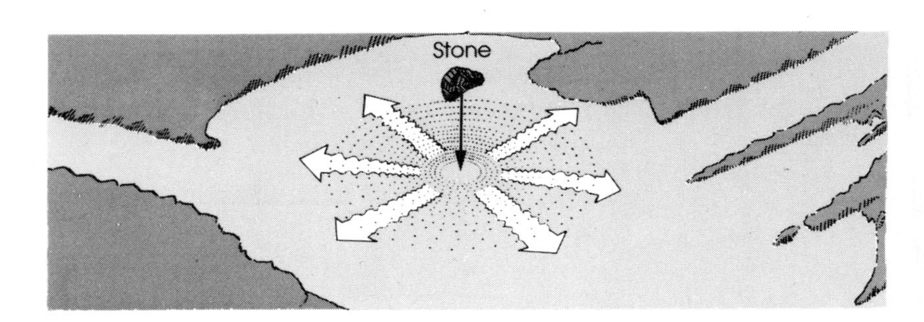


Ripples on a pond

## SOUND WAVES

If you drop a stone into the middle of a still pond, you can see ripples, or waves, travelling outwards away from the stone. These waves or ripples carry energy right across the pond. Sounds also travel in waves. They travel outwards, in every direction *away* from the vibrating object making the sound.

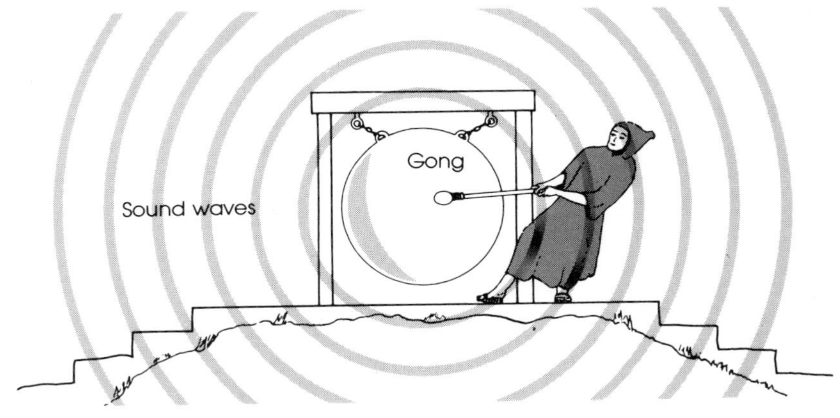


Sound travels outwards in all directions

You cannot see sound waves. But you can show the pattern of different sound waves on a special screen, like a television screen (the instrument used is described in Chapter 6). These pictures of sound waves can be used to compare different sounds:

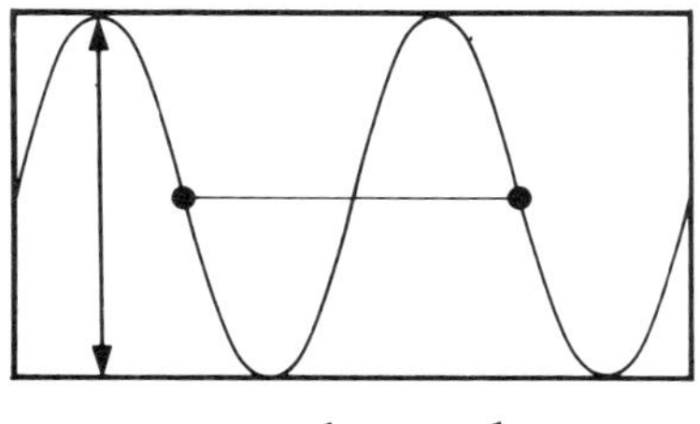

Loud sound

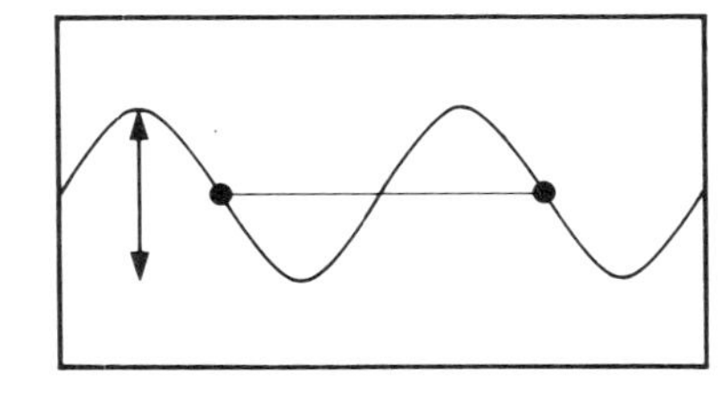

Softer sound, same pitch

The wave picture is higher for a loud sound than for a soft sound.

Two sounds may have exactly the same loudness but a different pitch:

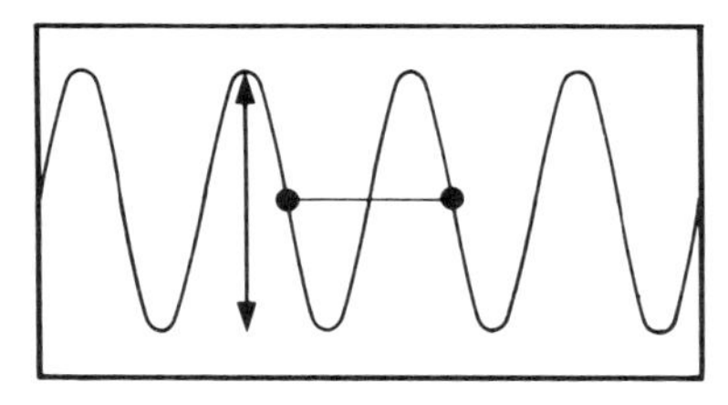

High pitch

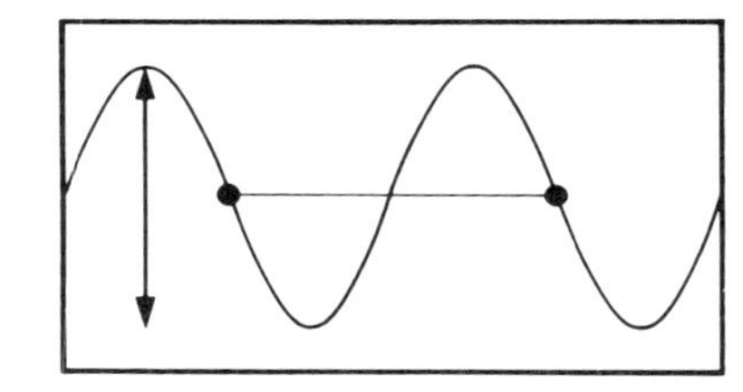

Lower pitch, same loudness

Here the waves for a high-pitched sound are closer together than for a lower-pitched sound.

ACTIVITY 5

## Unseen vibrations

Some vibrations cannot be seen. Tap a tuning fork gently so that it gives a musical note. Can you see the prongs of

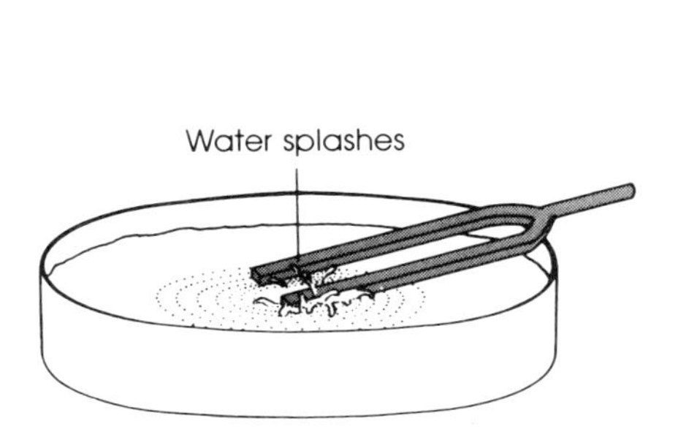


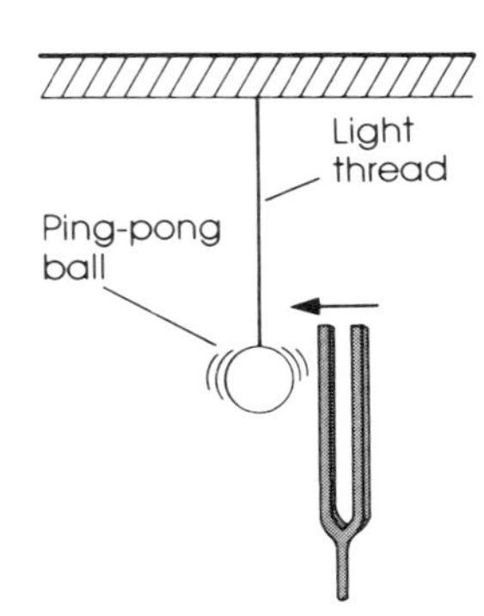

the fork vibrating? Now touch one prong against the surface of some water in a dish. What do you see?

Next, dangle a ping-pong ball on the end of a length of cotton. Touch one prong of a vibrating tuning fork against it. What happens? What do these experiments show?

## THE IMPORTANCE OF SOUNDS

People often forget how important sounds are in everyday life. Think of communications, for example. People communicate through sounds. They speak, shout, scream, groan, clap or just stay silent. Animals too use sounds to send messages: dogs bark or snarl; dolphins use a high-pitched whistle; birds have warning cries. Indeed many of the sounds that people hear are used as warnings. Imagine how much harder crossing the road would become if you were deaf.

Then think of the pleasure sounds can give. Speaking can be a *pleasant* way of communicating, and almost everyone enjoys listening to music — of some sort! Indeed most people have their favourite sounds — ranging from a gurgling stream to the sound of breaking glass.

Sometimes, sounds can be very useful — in industry, navigation, hospitals, fishing and even for spying. You can read about these uses in Chapter 7.

It is hard for someone who is not deaf to imagine life without sounds.

## QUESTIONS ON CHAPTER 1

**1** Supply words to fill in the blanks in this passage. Do not write on this page.
All sounds are made when something is ____. To-and-fro movements are examples of ____. Fast to-and-fro movements make ____ ____ sounds, slower movements make ____ ____ sounds. Sounds travel like ripples, or ____, across a pond. Sounds can be useful in ____ and in ____.

**2** There is a word to describe words like buzz, crack and pitter-patter. It has 13 letters which make the anagram 'I can moo too, pet!' The first two letters are 'on'. What is it?

# CHAPTER 2 TRAVELLING SOUNDS

## HOW DOES SOUND TRAVEL?

Sounds travel in waves. Try standing a row of dominoes on *edge,* close to each other. Give the first domino a push — the push travels like a wave along the row. Sounds travel in a similar way — in air and in many other materials.

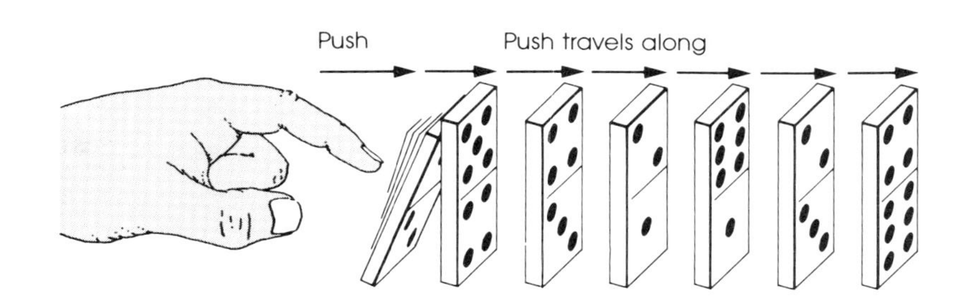


How to produce a domino wave

You already know that sounds are made by vibrating objects. Think of a tuning fork vibrating in air. As its prongs vibrate forwards, they push against the air next to them. Then, as the prongs vibrate backwards, the air next to them moves back again. These 'pushes' and 'pulls' travel through the air as a sound wave. The air is continually being

A tuning fork sending out a sound wave

*squashed* and *stretched* many times every second. The diagram at the bottom of p. 8 shows these 'squashes' and 'stretches' at different places along the sound wave. Notice that the sound wave travels *outwards,* in all directions, away from the vibration.

You can show how a sound wave travels with a special spring called a Slinky. Hold each end of the spring and extend it slightly. Now move one hand to and from slowly, into the spring and out again. You are continually pushing and pulling the spring, just like a vibrating object. These pushes and pulls can be seen travelling along the spring, just like the squashes and stretches in a sound wave.

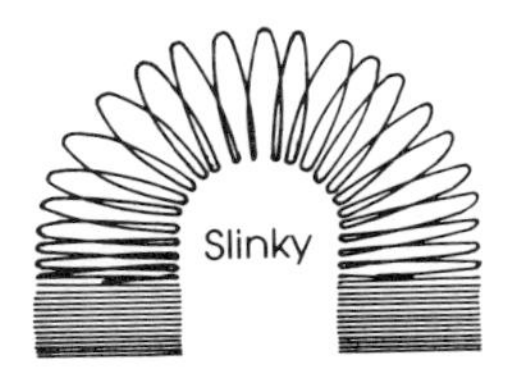


Waves on a Slinky

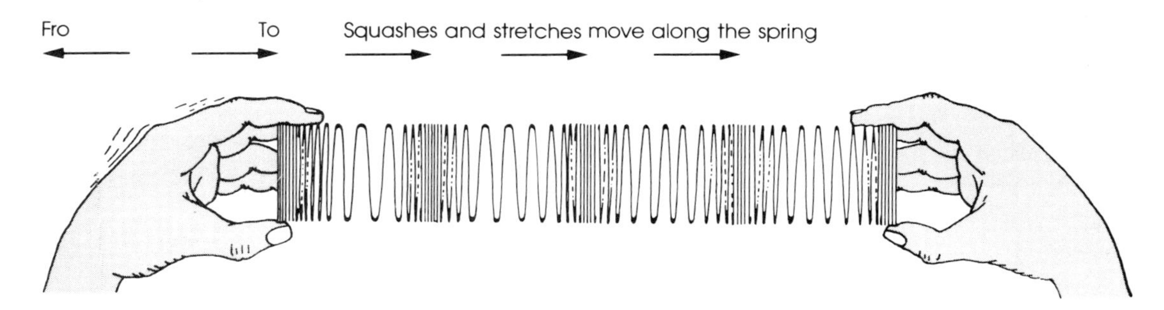


## WHAT HAPPENS TO THESE SOUND WAVES?

Sound waves can travel a long way. A bang on a radiator in a central heating system can travel right round a house. The sound of a horse's hooves can be heard over a mile away if you put your ear to the ground. But the further away you are from a vibration, the *weaker* the sound becomes. If someone blows a whistle close to you, your ears pick up quite a strong sound wave. But if you are 50 metres away, the sound wave is much weaker.

Sounds can travel a long way in air if they are not interrupted. But if a sound wave meets a hard, solid surface like a brick wall or a cliff, it bounces off. The sound wave is *reflected.* A reflected sound wave is called an *echo.* If you shout loudly about 20 metres from a high wall or a cliff, you can hear an echo. You hear the sound wave made by your own voice reflected off the cliff.

One famous place for echoes is the Whispering Gallery high in the dome of St. Paul's Cathedral. Any sound in the gallery is reflected again and again by the sides of the dome. A high-pitched whisper can be reflected many times, right around the gallery. A huge, white marble temple in India, called the Taj Mahal, can also keep any sound echoing for several seconds. Can you guess why?

The Whispering Gallery at St Paul's Cathedral

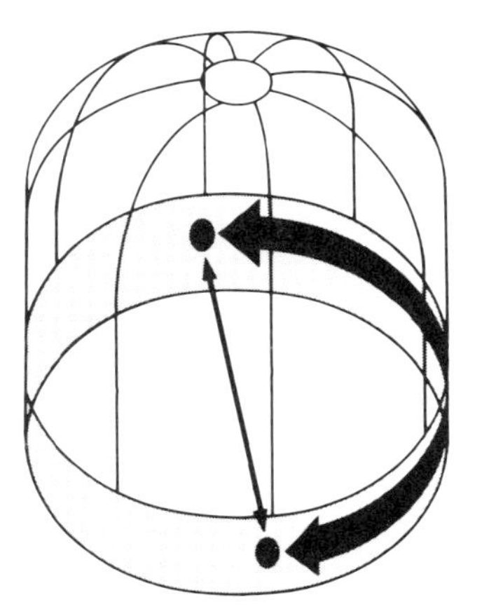

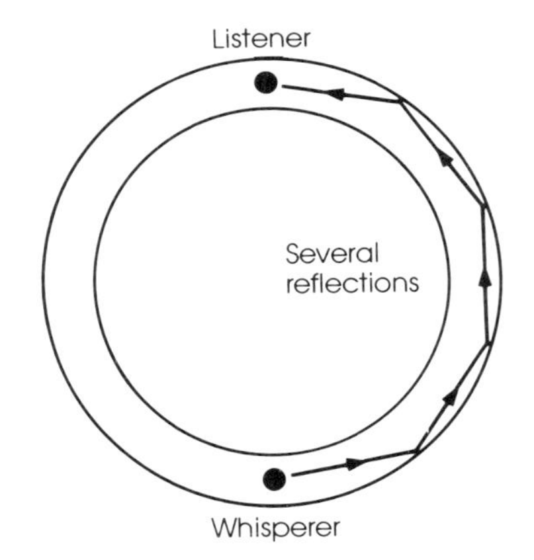


**ACTIVITY 6**

## Reflecting sounds

You need two cardboard tubes, a watch that ticks, two piles of books, a hard wall and a table. Put the watch just inside one tube. Lay this tube on one pile of books on the table at an angle to the wall.

Now lay the other tube on the second pile of books on the table with one end near the wall and your ear at the other. Slowly move this tube round until you hear the watch ticking. How does the sound reach you? Why do you need the piles of books? What do you notice about the angles between the tubes and the wall? Try this a few times with different angles.

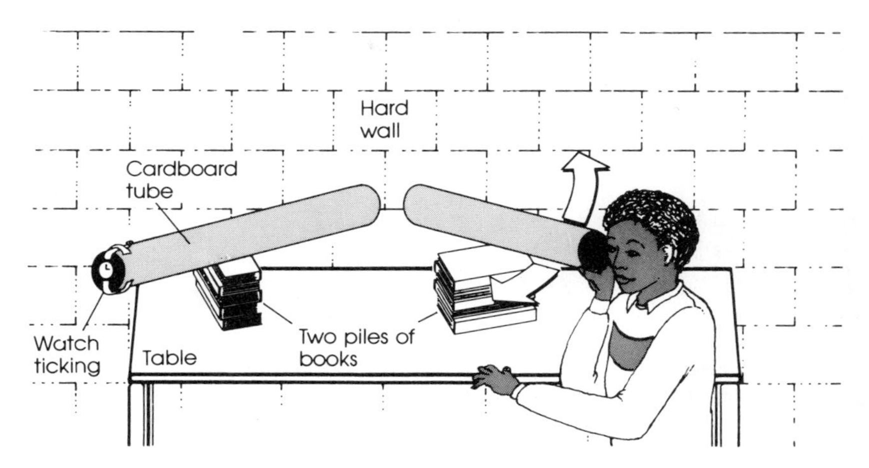


An experiment with reflecting sounds

## UNWANTED ECHOES

Echoes can be very useful (as we shall see in Chapter 7), but sometimes they are a nuisance. In a large concert hall, for example, the sound waves from musical instruments can echo round and round the building for a few seconds, spoiling the music. Because of this, most concert halls are planned to *absorb* or 'soak up' the reflected sound waves. Thick curtains and carpets, soft seats, padded walls, and even human beings and their clothes absorb sounds. The Royal Albert Hall in London uses special sound absorbers, hung from the ceiling. The study of sounds in halls, theatres, cinemas and all buildings is a subject in itself, called *acoustics*.

## WHICH MATERIALS CARRY SOUNDS?

Sound waves can travel through almost anything. They can travel through gases (such as air, carbon dioxide, helium and hydrogen). They can travel through liquids (such as fresh water and sea water). They can even travel through solids (such as brick, stone, skin, bone, wood, steel, glass and brass). But sounds cannot travel through a vacuum. They always need *something* to carry the squashes and stretches of a vibrating object.

ACTIVITY 7

## An experiment on sound in a vacuum

A well-known experiment is often used to show this. Place an electric bell inside a bell jar. Connect two wires from the bell to a battery and switch on. You can hear the bell ringing. Then remove as much air as you can from the jar using a vacuum pump. The sounds from the bell become fainter and fainter. Eventually you hear no sound although you can still *see* the bell ringing. (What does this tell you about light?)

Will sound travel through a vacuum?

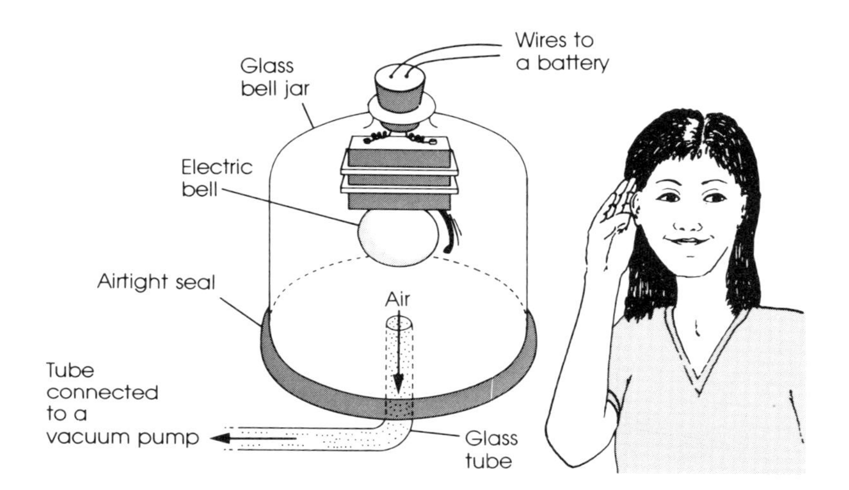


The fact that sound waves can travel through lots of different materials can be very useful:

1) Doctors can listen to your heart and lungs using a stethoscope — sound travels through your flesh, skin and bones.

2) The sea is an excellent material for carrying sound. Sound is absorbed many times *less* by water than by air. Ships use underwater sounds for navigation and submarines use them for detecting an enemy or an obstacle.

3) Some car mechanics use a stick touching the car engine to carry sounds to their ear to search for strange noises.

4) Nurses and doctors use ultrasonic sounds to 'see' the outline of an unborn baby in a mother's womb. The sound travels through the mother's skin and the protective fluid round the baby.

## SOUNDS IN SOLIDS AND LIQUIDS

Solids and liquids are excellent sound carriers.

**ACTIVITY 8**

### Listening in solids

Place your ear firmly on top of your desk. Now stretch your arm and knock gently on the other end. Can you hear the sound travelling through the wood? Now lift your ear by a few centimetres and knock again. How loud is the sound now?

Place your ear on the railing of a long iron fence. Ask someone to strike the fence with a stick about 10 metres away. You can hear the sound clearly through the fence. If you lift your ear slightly, you may be able to hear the sound through the iron *before* it reaches you through the air.

**ACTIVITY 9**

### Make your own hydrophone

An instrument used for detecting underwater sounds is called a *hydrophone.* You can make a simple one using three lengths of rubber tubing, a T-piece to connect them, a plastic funnel, and an old balloon or thin sheet of rubber.

Connect them up as the diagram shows. Get someone to bang two pieces of metal together under the water, tap the side of the sink, clang a bell, or make any underwater noise you like. What can you hear? If your hydrophone works, try it in a pond or a pool (but don't fall in).

A do-it-yourself hydrophone

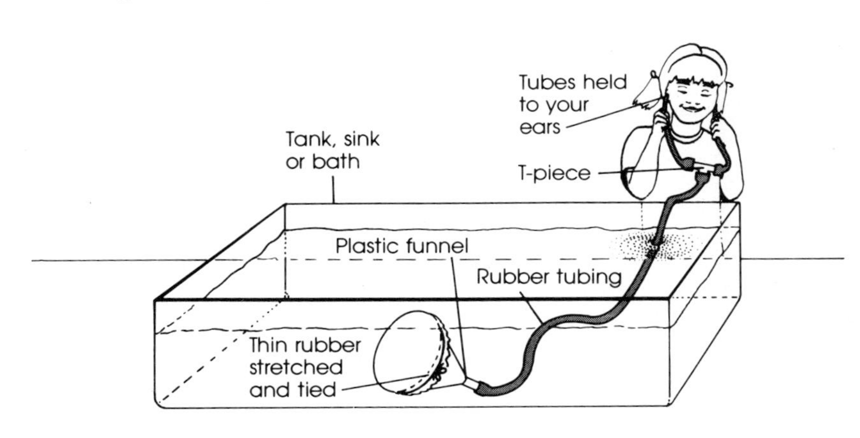


## HOW FAST DOES SOUND TRAVEL?

Sound travels at different speeds in different materials. In air, sound waves travel about 330 metres in *one second* — that's more than three times the length of a football pitch every second. Yet in water sound travels about four times as quickly — the speed of sound in water is about 1500 metres per second (or 1500 m/s). In solids, especially metals, sound travels even faster, for example, 3000 m/s in brick and 5000 m/s in steel. Because sound has so many different speeds there is no such thing as *the* speed of sound, even in air. Sound waves travel faster through warm air than through cold air.

## THE SPEED OF LIGHT AND THE SPEED OF SOUND

When you compare the speed of sound with everyday speeds like the speed of a sprinter or a fast car it seems very fast. Yet compared with the speed of light, the speed of sound is almost nothing. In 3 seconds, sound travels about *one kilometre* in air. In 3 seconds, light travels about *one million kilometres.* You can see examples of this in ever day life. If you watch someone a long way off knocking in a post, you *see* the bang before you hear it. At a cricket match you see the bat hit the ball before the noise reaches you. On a race track you see the starter's gun go off before you hear the bang.

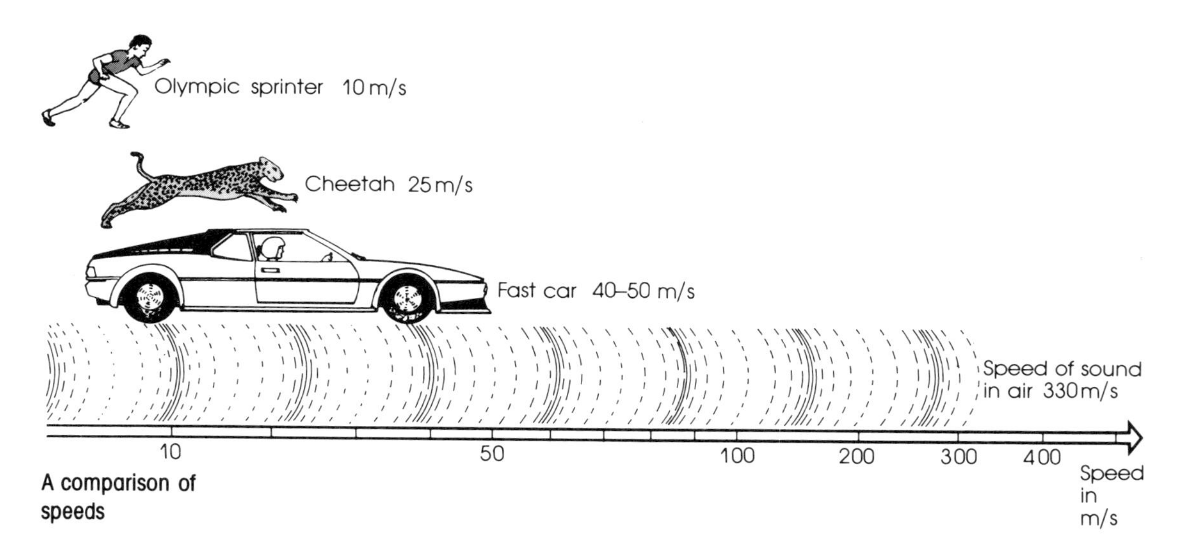

A comparison of speeds

You can use this difference during a thunderstorm to work out how far away the storm is. Measure the time between seeing the lightning flash and hearing the thunder. The time taken for the light to reach you is so small that you can ignore it, so what you are measuring is the time taken for the sound to reach you. For every 3 seconds, the storm is *1 kilometre* away. If, for example, the time taken is 12 seconds, the storm is 4 kilometres away. If the thunder and lightning come together, be thankful you are indoors!

## MEASURING THE SPEEDS OF SOUND

Nowadays we know the speeds of sound in different materials quite accurately. But how were they measured originally?

In 1708 a certain Mr Derham measured the speed of sound in air in London. His assistant fired a cannon on Blackheath. About 12½ miles (20 kilometres) away, in Upminster, Essex, Mr Derham sat on top of the church tower and listened for the bang. He saw the flash, then he heard the bang about 60 seconds later. This was the time taken for the sound to travel 20 kilometres. So

$$\text{the speed of sound} = \frac{20 \text{ kilometres}}{60 \text{ seconds}} = \frac{20\,000 \text{ metres}}{60 \text{ seconds}}$$

which roughly equals 330 metres per second.

A similar experiment was done on Lake Geneva in 1826 by two gentlemen called Colladon and Sturm. Colladon struck a bell under water and set off a flash at exactly the same instant. Sturm listened and watched in his rowing boat 9 miles away. The experiment was done at night so that Sturm could see the flash. He listened for the bell with a large ear trumpet under the water. The time gap between the flash and the clang of the bell was about 9 seconds. This meant that the sound had travelled about 9 miles in 9 seconds, or 1 mile in 1 second. The speed of sound in water had been measured: about 1 mile per second, or 1500 metres per second.

Colladon and Sturm's experiment. (a) A lever is pushed down to strike the bell and explode gunpowder at the same time. (b) About 9 miles away Sturm watches for the flash and listens for the clang

(a)

(b)

## BREAKING THE SOUND BARRIER

Some aeroplanes can fly faster than sound. Concorde can fly at 600 metres per second, about twice the speed of sound. Its engines make a lot of noise. When Concorde is flying quite slowly, *below* the speed of sound, the sound waves from its engines spread out in all directions away from the plane. But as Concorde speeds up it starts to catch up with its own sound waves! When it reaches the speed of sound, Concorde's sound waves cannot get away from the plane at all. Its sound waves collect together and bunch up just in front of the plane. As Concorde *passes* the speed of sound it actually overtakes its own sound waves. It breaks through 'the sound barrier'. This produces a very strong, sudden *boom* — a huge vibration called a *shock wave.* This is the sonic boom that you feel after the plane has gone by. Before you hear it you hear no noise from Concorde — it is travelling ahead of its own sound.

## QUESTIONS ON CHAPTER 2

**1** Supply words to fill in the blanks in this passage. Do not write on this page.
Sounds travel in ____. Reflected sounds are called ____. These can be ____ by thick carpets and padded seats. The study of sound in halls and theatres is called ____. Sounds can travel in gases, liquids and solids like ____, ____, and ____. Sounds travel more quickly in ____ than they do in air. The speed of sound in water is about ____ metres per second. When Concorde breaks the sound barrier it is followed by a ____ ____.

**2** Can you think of any buildings which make a lot of echoes? Can you explain why? Which type of materials are best for *reflecting* sound waves? Which kinds of material are best for *absorbing* them?

**3** When Mr Derham did his experiment to measure the speed of sound:

(a) What sort of day do you think was needed?

(b) On one day, with the wind in *one* direction, the time between the flash and the bang was 55½ seconds. On another day the time gap was 63 seconds. Which way do you think the wind was blowing on these two days? Why do you think the wind makes a difference?

**4** In Colladon and Sturm's experiment something unexpected happened. Sturm heard the first clang of the bell, then about half a minute later another *very faint clang* was heard. Can you explain why?

CHAPTER

3

# HEARING SOUNDS

## HOW DO YOU HEAR SOUNDS?

There are sounds everywhere. But they would be of no use to you if you couldn't *hear* them. Your body needs some way of changing sound waves into messages your brain can understand. This job is done by your *ears* — they convert sound waves into nerve impulses that travel to your brain. Your brain learns to interpret and *make sense* of these messages. Your brain gives *meaning* to the sounds you hear — the sounds of speech, warning sounds, sounds which are musical, and so on.

How you hear sounds

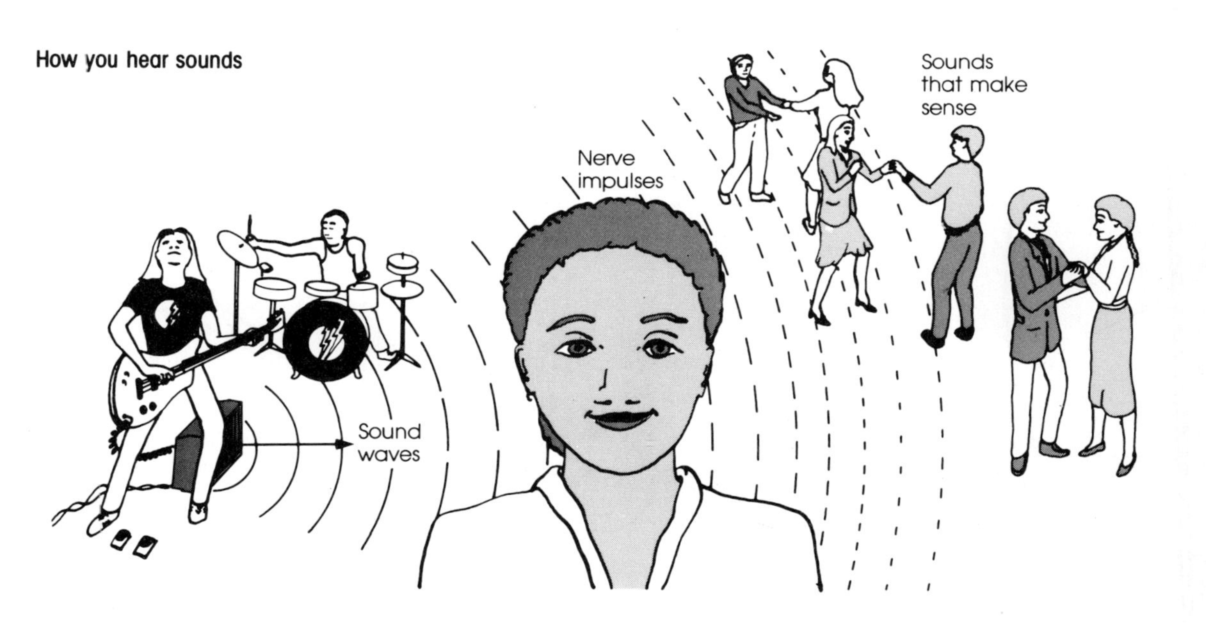


The parts of your ears you can see are two flaps of skin on the side of your head. Their job is really to *collect* sound waves. The important parts of your ear are hidden inside your skull for protection. The diagram on p. 18 shows the three different parts of your ear.

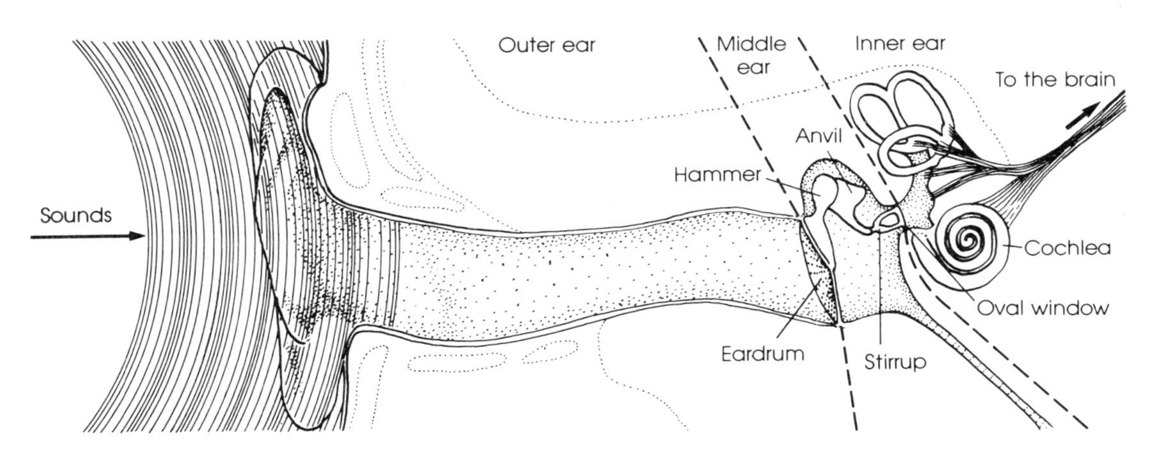


**The important parts of the ear**

Your outer ear is a flap of skin and a tube or canal to carry sound waves to your *eardrum.*

The middle ear is made up of three tiny bones. These are called the *hammer,* the *anvil* and the *stirrup* because of their shapes. When sound waves reach your eardrum it starts to vibrate, just like a drumskin. This touches the hammer, which carries the vibrations deeper into your ear through the three tiny bones. These bones carry or *conduct* the vibrations of your eardrum. But they also make the vibrations stronger — they *amplify* or magnify them. Finally, the inner-

**How the ear works**

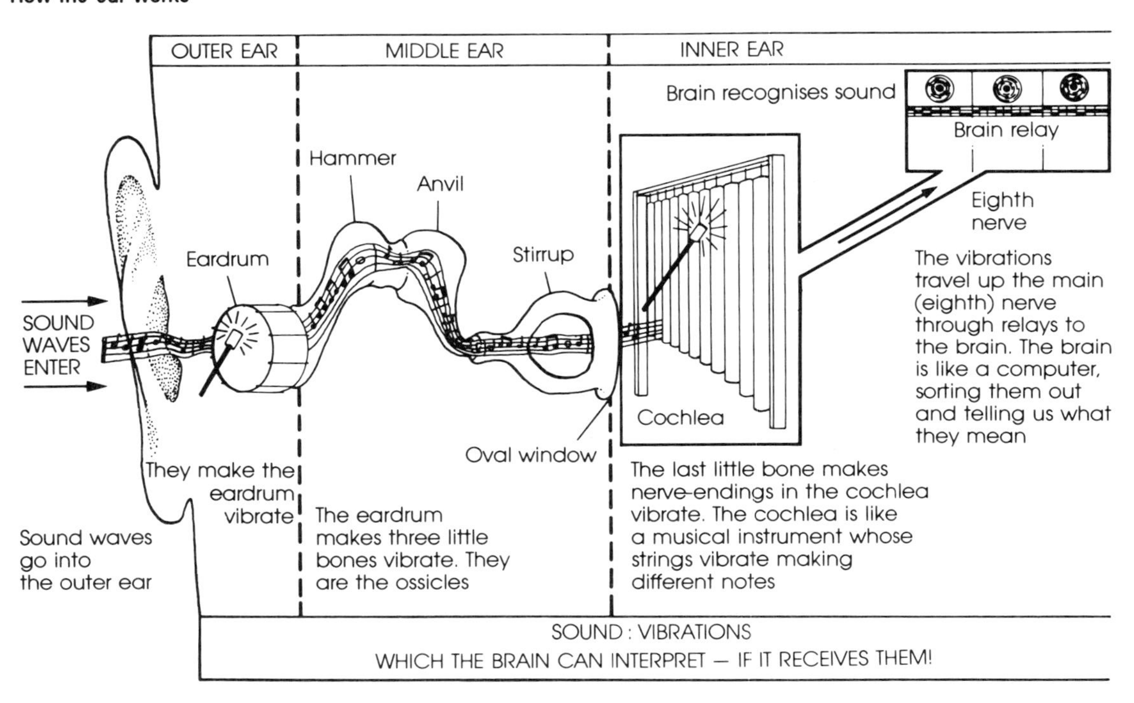

most bone (the stirrup) passes the vibrations on to your inner ear through an *oval window.* This is another piece of stretched skin, like your eardrum, which vibrates.

Behind the oval window is a coiled tube filled with liquid. This is called the *cochlea.* Inside it are thousands of tiny hairs. As the vibrations travel through the liquid they make *some* of these hairs vibrate. Scientists believe that different hairs vibrate for sounds of different *pitch.* When you hear a high-pitched sound, shorter hairs right inside the cochlea start to vibrate. With sounds of lower pitch, different hairs vibrate. These vibrating hairs send messages, or nerve impulses, to your brain. You *hear* a sound.

The diagram at the bottom of p. 18 shows the job done by different parts of your ear.

**ACTIVITY 10**

## Making a model eardrum

You will need a plastic carton or cup, a sharp knife or scalpel, and some very thin plastic such as 'cling wrap'. Carefully remove the bottom of the plastic carton, leaving no sharp edges. Stretch the cling wrap across it to make a tight film:

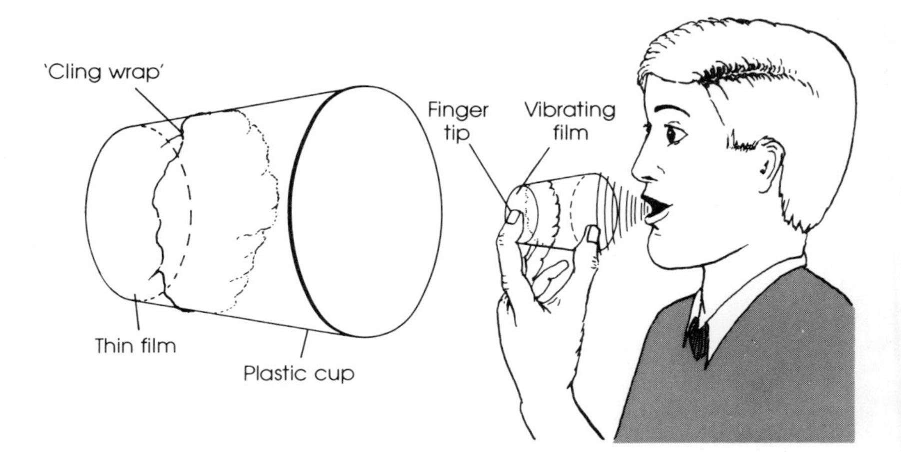


A model eardrum

Talk or sing into the open end. The film starts to vibrate, just like the membrane inside your ear. You can feel the vibrations by touching it lightly with your finger tips. You can show the vibrations by dangling a small polystyrene ball next to the cup. As the ball touches the film it jumps around:

How to demonstrate eardrum vibrations

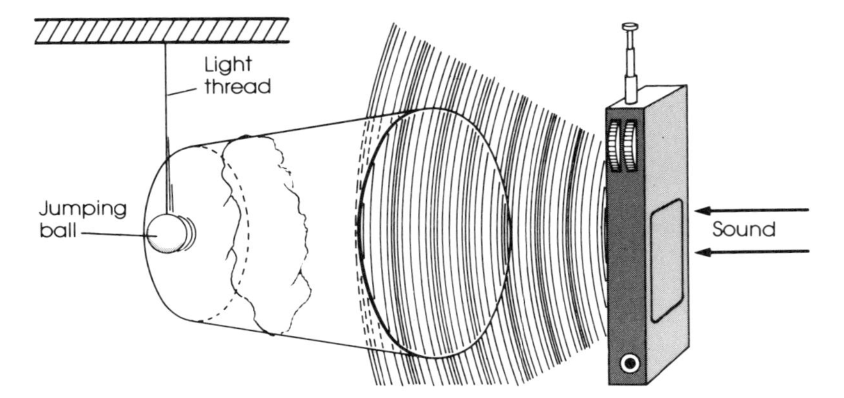


The sound can come from your voice, a radio, record player or television set.

Now make a tiny hole, for example, a pinprick, in the film. What effect does this have? Make a larger hole, say with a pencil. What happens now?

## WHICH SOUNDS CAN YOU HEAR?

Your ear sends different messages to your brain for sounds of different pitch. But there are sounds which your ear cannot hear. They may be too high, or too low.

There is another word for pitch: *frequency.* High-pitched sounds have a *high frequency,* low-pitched sounds have a *low frequency.* Sounds are caused by vibrations. The frequency of a sound depends on the frequency of its vibrations. Fast vibrations give high-frequency sounds; slow vibrations give low-frequency sounds.

Frequency is measured by the number of vibrations every second. One vibration per second is called a *hertz,* Hz for short; 20 vibrations per second is called 20 hertz (20 Hz); 256 vibrations per second is 256 Hz, and so on.

Very few people can hear sounds with a frequency *higher* than 20 000 Hz, and few people can hear sounds *lower* than 20 Hz. These are the limits of hearing, but they vary from person to person.

**ACTIVITY 11**

### Finding your hearing limits

You can find your own limits, as follows. Connect a loudspeaker to a signal generator (an instrument that can make sounds of different frequency). Start with a very low frequency that you cannot hear (just below 20 Hz). Gradually raise the frequency until *you just hear* the note from the speaker. This is your lower limit. Now steadily raise the frequency of the note. Its pitch gets higher and higher. Suddenly you stop hearing it. This is your upper limit.

Different people have different upper and lower limits. Young people can hear sounds across a wider range than adults can. Animals have a very different range of hearing.

## WHICH SOUNDS CAN ANIMALS HEAR?

Dogs can easily hear sounds that are beyond our hearing. Their upper limit is about 50 000 Hz. Some dog whistles use this difference — these whistles are silent to us, but dogs respond to them and come running. Bats and porpoises can hear sounds of even higher frequency. The sounds in their world are as high as 100 000 Hz, the world of 'ultrasounds'.

The table below shows the different sounds that animals and instruments can *make* — and also the sounds and frequencies that different animals can *hear*.

Frequencies made and heard

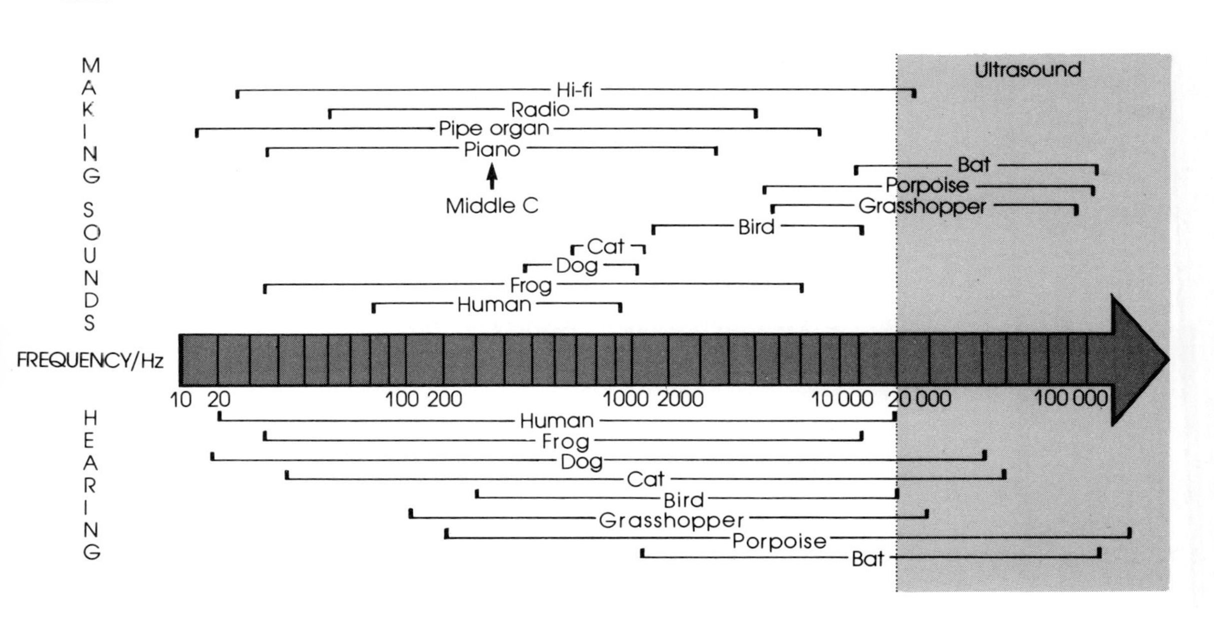


## HOW CAN HEARING GO WRONG?

Many people have problems with their hearing. *Partial deafness* is not uncommon, but it is often unnoticed. Some people, often old people, are just 'slightly hard of hearing'. But many children have poor hearing. In the past, teachers might have thought these children slow or not very clever.

Nowadays most children have their hearing tested when they are babies, but many doctors feel that hearing tests, like eye tests, should be used more often.

The word 'deafness' is used to describe very many different conditions. Many people are partially deaf. Some people are born deaf. Some people are totally deafened by an accident. Others are made partially deaf by continual noise at work. One type of deafness occurs when people cannot hear sounds of certain frequencies. Their ears cannot hear sounds of high frequency — this makes it hard for them to understand speech, especially sounds like *t* and *s*.

Different types of deafness have different *causes.* Some children in the past were born deaf because their mothers had German measles and the delicate parts of the inner ear never developed properly. Fortunately this is rarer now.

Some people have their eardrums damaged by an accident. An extremely loud noise can 'burst' someone's eardrum. A sharp object pushed into the ear can make a hole or *perforate* it. This is why sharp objects should *always* be kept away from the ears.

More and more people are becoming partially deaf through continual noise at work, or noise at pop concerts or discotheques. The dangers of different noise levels are explained on p. 40.

Many people become partially, and sometimes totally deaf, after an illness. Any kind of ear infection can damage your hearing. But serious illnesses, like meningitis or scarlet fever, or even measles, can cause deafness.

## TYPES OF DEAFNESS

Most forms of deafness occur because sound waves never even *reach* the inner ear. They are not carried through or *conducted* to the inner ear. This deafness results from a damaged eardrum, or perhaps damaged bones in the middle ear. Deafness in old people is usually caused by the bones in their middle ear not vibrating properly. This type of deafness is called *conductive deafness.*

The other type of deafness is more serious and is incurable. This deafness affects either the cochlea or the auditory nerve. Their job is to make and send messages or nerve impulses to the brain. If these messages are not made, or not sent, *nerve deafness* results.

## HOW CAN POOR HEARING BE HELPED?

As yet there is no way of curing nerve deafness, because scientists have not discovered a way of changing sound waves into nerve impulses.

Although scientists cannot copy the job done by the inner ear, they can help the outer and middle ears to do *their* job — the job of carrying or conducting sound waves to the inner ear. Sound waves can be collected and carried to your ear with a simple *ear trumpet.* Modern hearing aids use a microphone to pick up sound waves. These are magnified or amplified by an amplifier, and then fed into the person's ear through a tiny earphone. An earphone is just a small loudspeaker.

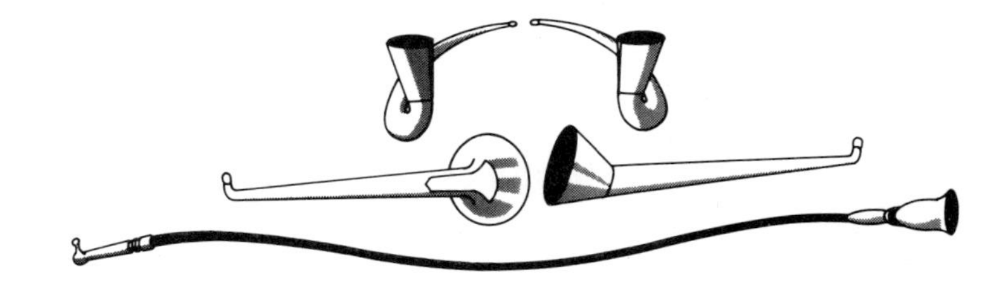

Various old-fashioned hearing aids

The hearing aid also needs a tiny battery, a switch and a volume control. But the whole thing can now be made very, very small. The electric circuit for the amplifier can be formed into a tiny wafer or 'chip' of silicon. The complete hearing aid can be hidden behind a person's ear.

Hearing aids help to magnify sound waves and carry them into someone's ear. But some people who are partially deaf can actually hear sounds *through their skull.* Some claim that they can hear sounds through their teeth. An American called Thomas Edison invented the first gramophone in 1877. He became more and more deaf as he grew older, due to an earlier accident. Edison listened to his new invention through his skull and his teeth:

> 'If I place my head against my gramophone I can hear the musical notes. When I bite hard against the case I feel the music more and more strongly.'

The bones in your skull can carry or *conduct* the sounds to your inner ear almost as well as the hammer, the anvil and the stirrup do.

ACTIVITY 12

### Hearing through your bones

Hold the stem of a vibrating tuning fork gently against your skull, then your temple, then your jawbone. How well do you hear it? Now hold the vibrating tuning fork a few inches away from your head. How well do you hear it now? What does this activity show?

ACTIVITY 13

### Why do you have two ears?

You need a circle of friends, two short pieces of wood or a bell, and a blindfold. Form your friends into an even circle around the room. Stand one person at a time in the middle of the circle with a blindfold on. Then, one person taps the wooden pieces sharply together, or rings the bell. The person wearing the blindfold has to guess correctly who made the noise (a bit like blind man's buff). How well did you score?

Now do exactly the same again, with each person in turn. But *this* time the blindfolded person in the middle covers one ear completely, for example, by putting a finger in one ear. How does this affect the results? Now explain why people have two ears.

## QUESTIONS ON CHAPTER 3

**1** Supply words to fill in the blanks in this passage. Do not write on this page.
A human ear consists of three parts called the ____ ear, the ____ ear, and the ____ ear. There are three tiny bones in the ____ ear called the hammer, the ____ and the ____. Three bones carry sound waves into the ____ ear through the ____ window. Deep inside your ear there is a tube coiled like a snail's shell called the ____. This converts sound waves into ____ ____ for the brain.

**2** Draw a diagram of the three parts of a human ear and label the important bits. What job does each part do?

**3** What is the difference between conductive deafness and nerve deafness? Explain how one type of deafness can be helped, but not the other.

CHAPTER

4

# SPEAKING

## WHERE DOES YOUR VOICE COME FROM?

All sounds are made by vibrations. Your voice can make sounds: laughing, singing, shouting, screaming. So what is vibrating?

Inside your body is a tube that carries air from your mouth to your lungs. This is your *windpipe.* Inside your windpipe are two flaps of skin called *vocal chords.* These are contained in a sort of 'box' called your *larynx* or voice box (this is just behind the lump in your throat that people call your Adam's apple). When the vocal chords vibrate your voice makes a sound.

What makes them vibrate? Your brain can control your vocal chords. When you want to make a sound your brain sends a message which pulls your vocal chords partly *across* your windpipe. You then breathe air out from your lungs. This moving air pushes against the chords in your windpipe and makes them vibrate.

Your brain can control these vibrating vocal chords in many different ways. You can make high or low sounds, loud or soft sounds, long or short sounds.

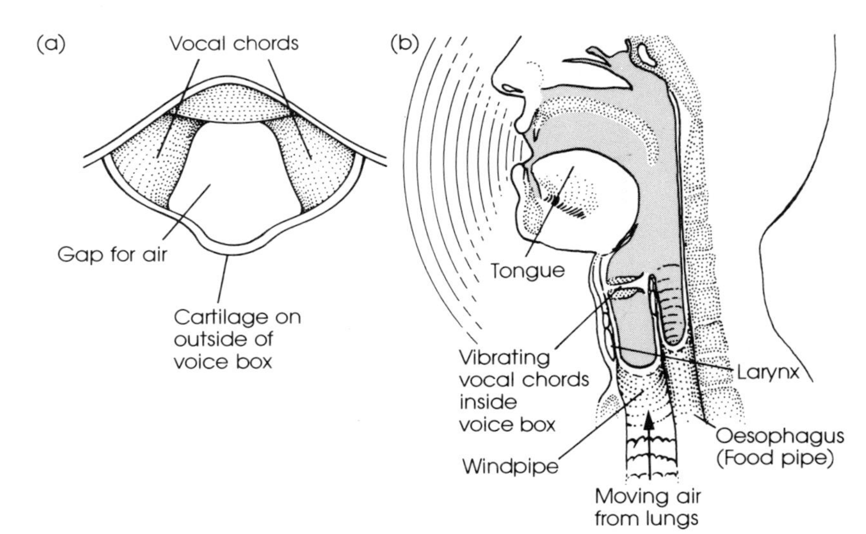


The vocal chords.
(a) Looking down the windpipe from above.
(b) A view from the side

**ACTIVITY 14**

### Making model vocal chords

Tie a piece of old balloon across the end of a cardboard tube as tightly as you can (see the diagram). Cut a narrow slit across the centre of the balloon. Now blow into the other end of the tube.

The balloon vibrates just as your vocal chords do. The tube is like your windpipe. Why do you need a slit? What might happen if thicker rubber were used?

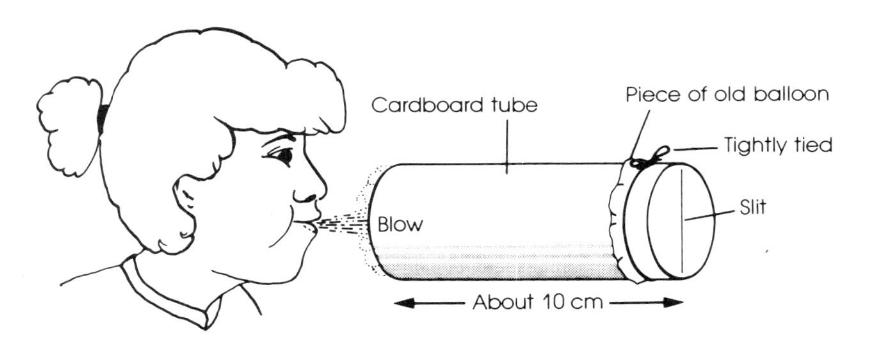


Model vocal chords

## HOW DO YOU MAKE DIFFERENT SOUNDS?

When you want to make a high-pitched sound your brain stretches your vocal chords. It makes them *just tight* enough to make the sound you want. Your brain can also make your vocal chords slacker or looser. Loosely stretched vocal chords vibrate more slowly and make lower notes.

The other thing which changes the *pitch* of the sounds you make is the *length* of your vocal chords. Your brain cannot do this. *Growth* does it for you. Your vocal chords are very short as a baby, less than 3 mm. As you get older your vocal chords grow. When a boy matures his voice 'breaks' and his vocal chords get longer and thicker. A man's vocal chords may be as long as 30 mm.The human voice can vary in pitch from a low note of 80 Hz to a high one of 1100 Hz.

The *loudness* of the sounds you make depends on the force of the air from your lungs pushing on them. To make a loud sound your lungs push air past your vocal chords at great speed. The vocal chords then vibrate strongly. To make quiet sounds your lungs expel less air, more slowly. When you sing, your voice can hold a *quiet* note for longer than a *loud* note — the air is pushed out more slowly from your lungs. Try it for yourself.

Different sounds have a different *power* — this is a measure of the energy they need every second. A whisper has a power of about 0.001 microwatts (one microwatt is one millionth of a watt). A loud scream can have a power of about 500 microwatts. These powers seem quite small when you compare then with the power of an average light bulb: about 60 watts.

The human voice is able to make many different sounds by 'moulding' them. Examples are: *ooh, aah, eeh, th, b* and *f.* You can do this by controlling different parts of your body, from the lungs upwards: your lips, your mouth, your jaws, your tongue, and your palate (the roof of your mouth).



## SOUNDS OF SPEECH

The different sounds you make when you are speaking depend mainly on where you put your *tongue.* Try saying a *d* or a *t.* Where did you put your tongue? You should feel it touching the back of your front teeth. Here are the positions of your tongue for other sounds:

*th*: your tongue is between your lips and your teeth.
*sh* and *s*: you make an 'air channel' along the middle of your tongue.

You also use your lips to make different sounds in speech. Try looking at your lips in the mirror when you say *s, b, p, th, eeh,* or *aah.* The diagram below shows the different lip shapes for different sounds. You can see that your teeth are important too — when you say *f* or *v* your top teeth touch your lower lip.

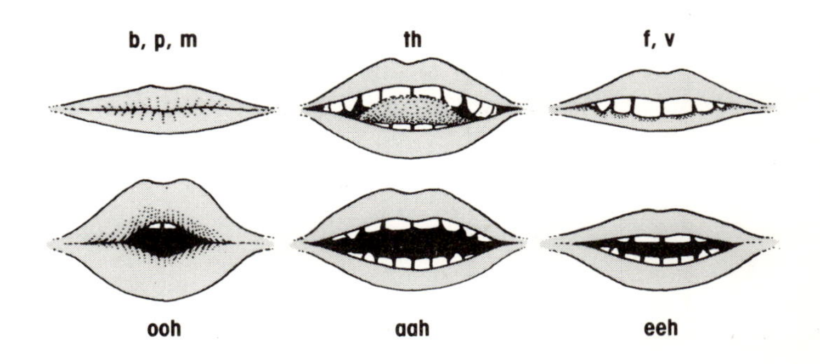


Lip shapes for different sounds

You may notice that your lips are exactly the same for the sounds *b* and *p.* So why are they different sounds? Try saying *b* with two fingers holding your voice box. You can feel your vocal chords vibrate. This is called a voiced sound. Now do the same for the sound *p* (as in 'plate'). This time your vocal chords *do not vibrate.* A sound like *p* is called an unvoiced sound — it does not use your vocal chords. The table below shows some voiced and unvoiced sounds.

**Voiced and unvoiced sounds**

| *Voiced* | *Unvoiced* |
|---|---|
| *b* | *p* |
| *d* | *t* |
| *g* | *k* |
| *z* | *s* |
| *j* | *ch* |

Each pair uses the same lip and tongue movements

The great variety of sounds that you make in speech depends not only on your tongue, lips and teeth but on the shape of the passages and cavities in your mouth, nose and throat. The study of speech is now seen as a science in itself, *speech science.*

In fact, speech is one thing that makes human beings different from other animals. Animals can make noises, but as far as we know they don't talk to each other.

**ACTIVITY 15**

## Making a tin-can telephone

You need two empty tin cans (watch out for sharp edges) and a long length of string, up to five metres if possible. Make a small hole in the bottom of each can. Thread the string through these two holes and tie two small knots.

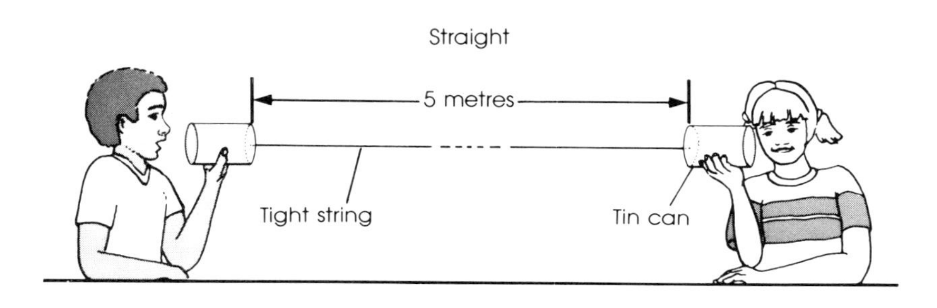


The tin-can telephone

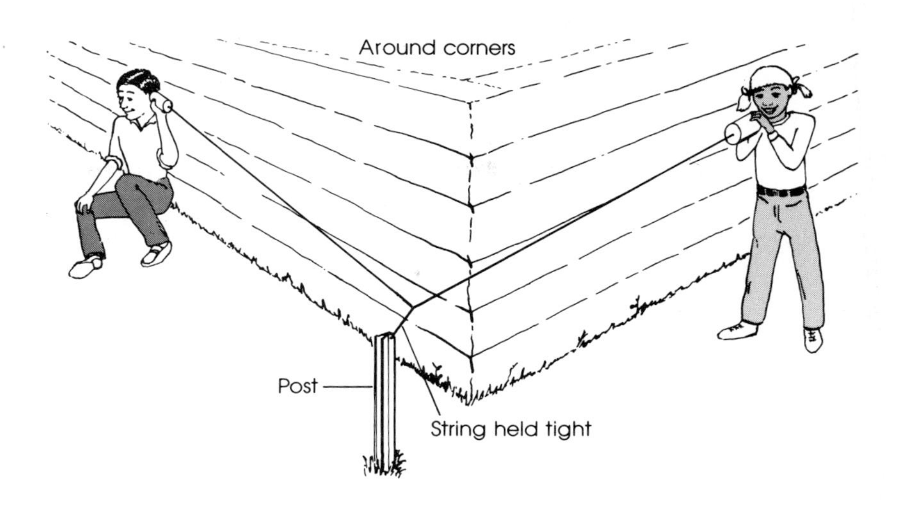


This is a 'string telephone'. Always keep the string tight. (Do you know why?)

How does the sound travel from one can to the other? What does this experiment show?

**ACTIVITY 16**

## Making a megaphone

You need a sheet of cardboard, a pair of scissors, and some sticky tape.

Make the cardboard into a cone. Talk though the narrow end, and ask someone to listen. What do you notice? Can you explain what is happening?

The megaphone and how it works

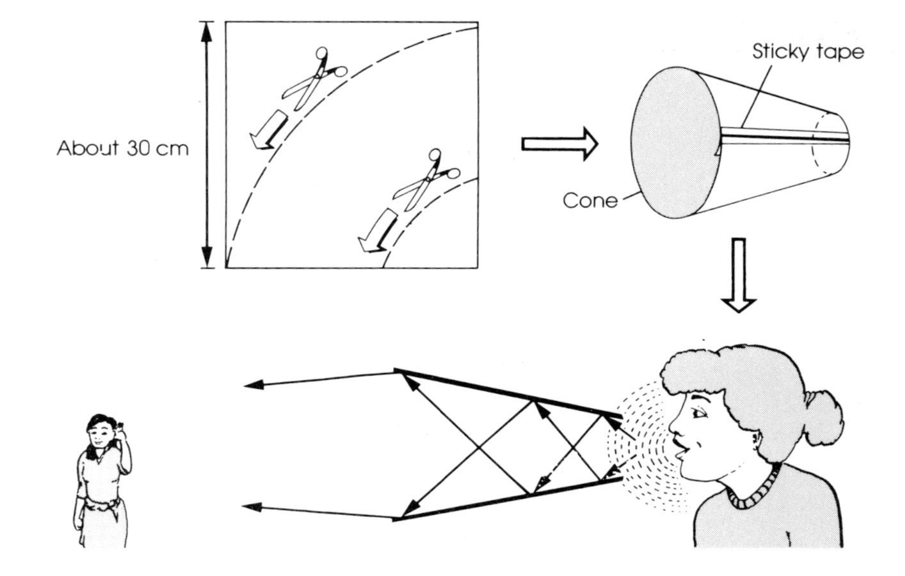

## ANIMAL NOISES

Many animals *communicate* with each other by sounds. A blackbird makes a warning call to signal danger. Other birds, like the seagull, use their warning call to say 'keep off'. Singing birds like the warbler or a nightingale may use their voice to attract a mate of the opposite sex.

Many fish make, and hear, sounds. Indeed water is an excellent substance to live in if sounds are important. More intelligent fish (such as porpoises) certainly send messages to each other (see p. 21). Tadpoles can hear in water, but when they develop into frogs their ears change too. A frog's ears have eardrums like ours, which pick up vibrations in air. A male frog 'croaks' to a female by puffing out its throat to make a large *vocal sac.* Air travels to and fro between this sac and the frog's lungs to make the croaking sound. Try croaking yourself.

Insects make sounds in strange ways. Grasshoppers and crickets scrape their back leg, which is rough like a saw, against a wing. This makes the scraping sound you may have heard in the country on a summer evening. The fast-moving wings of many insects make a 'hum' or a 'buzz' as the air vibrates. You often hear this humming but not many insects do. Most insects are deaf.

The giraffe makes no noise.

## QUESTIONS ON CHAPTER 4

**1** Supply words to fill in the blanks in this passage. Do not write on this page.
The tube that carries air to your lungs is called the ____.
Inside this tube are two flaps of skin called ____ ____.
These are contained in your ____ ____.

**2** Make a table showing the different parts of your body used to make your voice, and the job that each part does. Which parts do you control to make the different sounds in speech?

**3** Read this passage. Then talk about it and try to answer the questions.

# VOICE PRINTS

It is now possible to make a picture of a person's voice. This picture is called a voice print, or sound *spectrogram.*

A voice print is made by recording all the different frequencies that together make up a person's voice. The sum total of these frequencies is different for each individual. So everyone's voice print, like their fingerprint, is different. Your voice is your own.

Voice prints

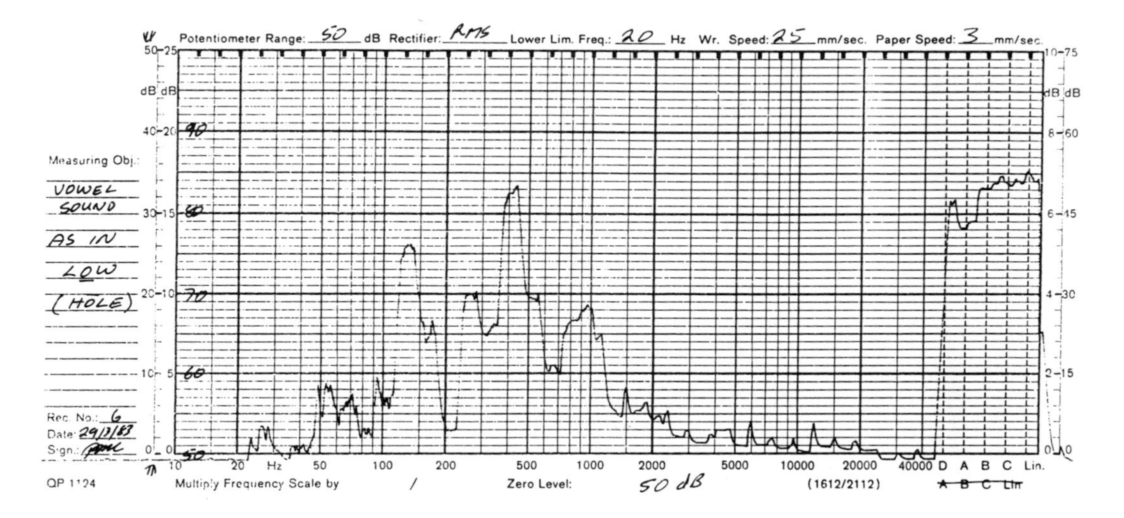


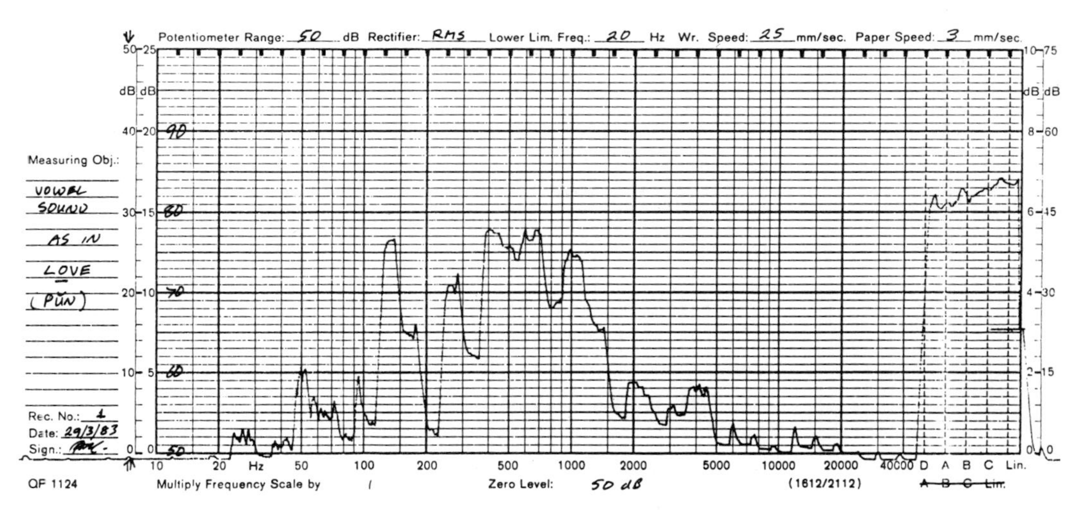


Some police forces now use voice prints to identify criminals. Can you see any advantages in this? Do you think they would be better, or worse, than fingerprints? Explain some ways in which fingerprints are more useful for catching criminals than voice prints.

CHAPTER 5

# WHAT A RACKET!

## WHAT IS NOISE?

Have you ever been accused of making too much of a din? 'Keep that noise down' is a common cry. But sounds which are *noise* to some people are *music* to others. So just what is noise?

Noises are unwanted sounds. You may want them, but someone else may not. Loud conversations, the roar of a football crowd, music, squawking seagulls or simply running water can be noises just because they are unpleasant to someone.

## NOISE POLLUTION

Most people associate 'pollution' with dirty rivers, dead fish, smoky air or oily sea. Noise pollution occurs whenever there are sounds around which make life unpleasant. It may come from traffic, factory machines, aeroplanes taking off, a discotheque, a loud television or a noisy party.

Although the expression 'noise pollution' is new, annoying noises have been around for a long time. In the eighteenth century the streets of London were probably as noisy as they are today — though the noises would have been quite different.

These days, there are doctors who study the damaging effects of noise. American doctors have shown how *tiring* noise can be — a typist in a noisy office wastes one-fifth of her energy just putting up with the din. People who visit London for the day often feel 'worn out', partly because of noise pollution.

Noises can literally drive people mad. A few years ago a man in Berwick-upon-Tweed was woken up late one night by noisy partygoers in the street. When he went out to ask for quiet they chased him back into his house. The man picked up his shotgun, killed two people and wounded two others. His charge was reduced to manslaughter.

Doctors realised that noise can make annoyance, frustration and anger build up inside people. They discovered that noise pollution was creating tension, stress, and even sickness in thousands of people. In 1959 the Noise Abatement Society was founded by John Connell. He was particularly worried about the effects of noises on children:

> 'Young people have become conditioned to demanding very loud amplified music for listening and dancing. They like it, and can be expected to object to any reduction in volume and vibration, so we are going to expect some difficulty in reversing the trend. But reverse it we must if we are going to absolve ourselves of the responsibility for producing the Deaf Generation.'

He said this in 1959. Music has become a lot louder since. Do you think of yourself as part of the Deaf Generation?

John Connell, founder of the Noise Abatement Society

## MEASURING NOISE

It is the loudest noises that make most noise pollution. The loudness of noises, and sounds, is measured in *decibels.* On this scale a sound is compared with the quietest sound that most people's ears can hear — this is called the *threshold of audibility,* and has a loudness of 0 decibels. When people

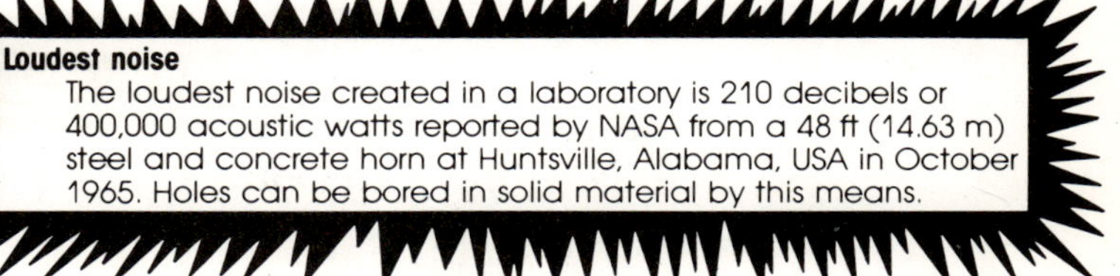

**Loudest noise**
The loudest noise created in a laboratory is 210 decibels or 400,000 acoustic watts reported by NASA from a 48 ft (14.63 m) steel and concrete horn at Huntsville, Alabama, USA in October 1965. Holes can be bored in solid material by this means.

Extract from **The Guinness Book of Records**

talk to each other the sounds have a loudness of between 40 and 60 decibels. A noisy discotheque can reach 100 decibels, while sounds above 140 decibels can be quite painful. The loudest voice in 1982, that of a Yorkshireman, reached a level of 112 decibels.

Some sounds above 160 decibels can actually burn human skin or bore holes in a brick.

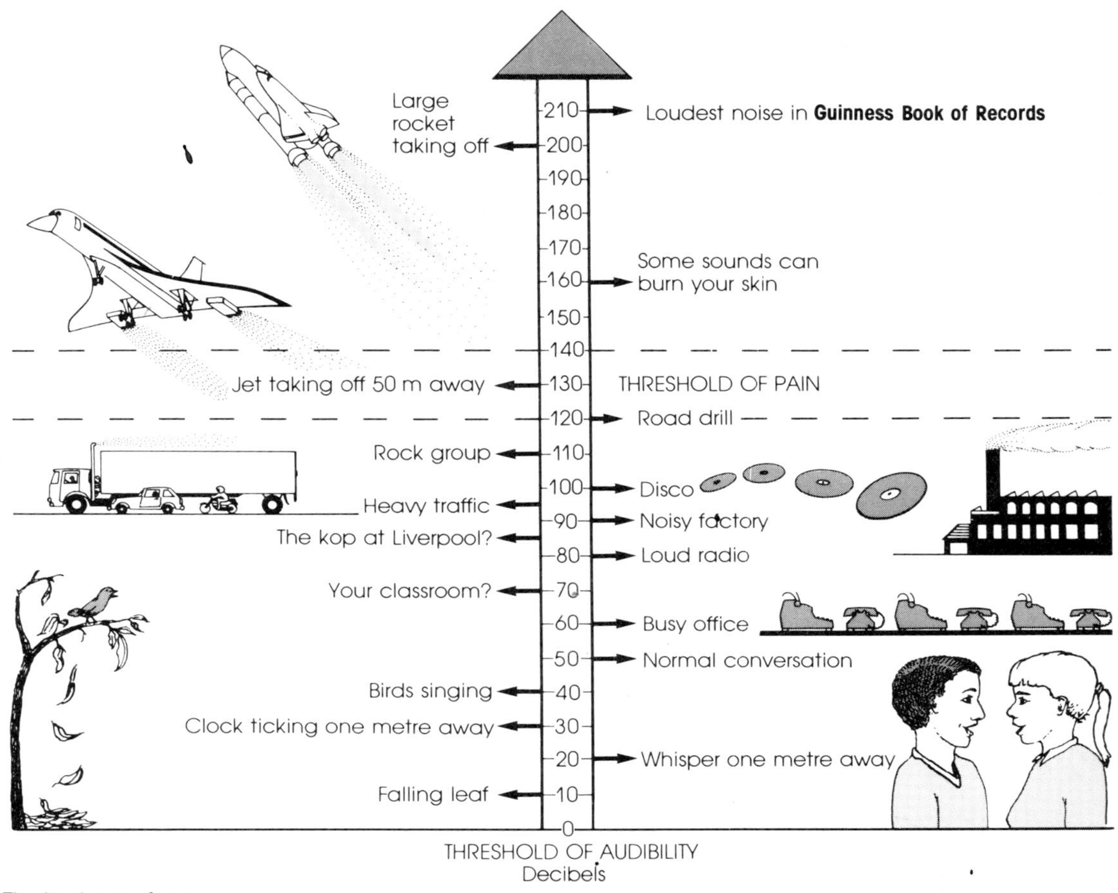


The loudness of some common noises

## NOISE METERS

How can you measure loudness? Special meters called 'sound level meters' are used nowadays. These can be held in your hand and pointed at the sound. Old-fashioned noise meters used a thin membrane a bit like your eardrum. This was connected by a delicate thread to a pen. As the sound reached the membrane it started to vibrate, which made the pen move and trace a wavy line on a piece of paper.

As you can guess, this was very inaccurate. The main part of

A meter for measuring noise

a modern sound meter is the microphone. This changes the vibrations from a sound wave into tiny pulses of electricity. These electrical pulses can be carried to a voltmeter which is calibrated in decibels. Sometimes they can be sent to an oscilloscope to make a wavy trace on a screen. The height of the wave gives you an idea of its loudness.

A hiss and a rumble on an oscilloscope screen

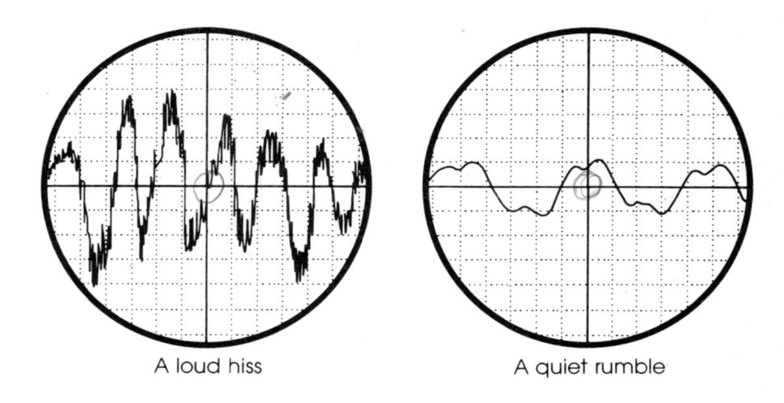

A loud hiss

A quiet rumble

ACTIVITY 17

## Using a noise meter

If you can borrow a sound meter try measuring some different noise levels. For example:

The noise beside a busy road
The noise on a country lane
The noise inside your classroom
The noise inside a discotheque
The noise of a train passing by.

You could measure the levels of many other noises, depending on where you live.

How do you think the noise levels change with the time of day?

## TYPES OF NOISE POLLUTION

Traffic noise comes from various sources: the tyres on the road, the engine, the exhaust system, and so on. In almost every city traffic noise is the biggest cause of noise pollution. The noise from a heavy lorry passing close by can reach 80 or 90 decibels; the loudness of sounds from buses can be as high as 85 decibels; the noise level of most cars is between 70 and 80 decibels.

Noise levels from aircraft are much higher. This table shows the noise heard from a few types of aeroplane if you are 300 metres away.

| *Plane* | *Noise level at 300 m in decibels* | |
|---|---|---|
| | *Take-off* | *Landing* |
| Propeller planes e.g. F-27, DC-3 | 85–90 | 75–80 |
| Smaller jets e.g. Boeing-707, DC-8 | 100–105 | 95–100 |
| Large jets e.g. Boeing-747 | 105 | 90 |

Thousands of people have to face noisy factories every day — noise from pumps, ventilators, drills, saws, and all kinds of other machines. One international organisation has said that workers should not be exposed to noise levels above 90 decibels for a working day. But doctors already know that noise levels over 80 decibels for *long* periods can damage your hearing — so this limit is much too high. Thousands of factory workers are already *partially* deaf.

Even enjoying music can be dangerous. The average sound level in a discotheque is about 103 decibels — in a rock concert it can reach 120 decibels near the stage, just below the pain threshold. Many pop musicians and D.J.s suffer partial deafness (described on p. 22).

If you watch car racing, beware! The noise at the trackside from Formula 1 racing cars can reach 115 decibels.

## KEEPING THE NOISE DOWN

We have all these noises about us — from traffic, aeroplanes, factories and even leisure activities. Yet a 'healthy' noise level for people to live in is about 45 decibels (day time) and 35 decibels (night-time). So how can noise levels be reduced? There are three places where noise pollution can be tackled:

1) at the source of the noise, for example, by using quieter machines, making cars and planes quieter
2) as the noise travels, for example, by absorbing the noise
3) at the place where you hear sound — your ears.

Advice from The Royal Society for the Prevention of Accidents

To some extent people can help themselves. Those who make noise should be more aware of the effect it has on others. Car and lorry drivers, for example, can keep noise down by quieter driving — not revving their engines, accelerating and braking less sharply, and driving more slowly in built-up areas. People who work in factories or discotheques can help themselves by wearing earmuffs. But people who *plan* towns and cities can do the most to help. Roads can be screened from houses by walls and trees. New housing estates can be built away from heavy traffic. Airports and residential areas can often be kept separate.

Even so, plans can go wrong. There are hundreds of people who live too close to an airport. Soundproofing is their only answer. The problem is that sound can travel through any material — glass, brick, stone, air, water, even steel. Only a perfect vacuum can stop it completely. However, some materials are good at *absorbing* the energy of sounds.

You know from p. 8 that sounds are carried by something vibrating. The noise of an aeroplane is carried by vibrating air. Where these air vibrations reach a closed window they

Windows

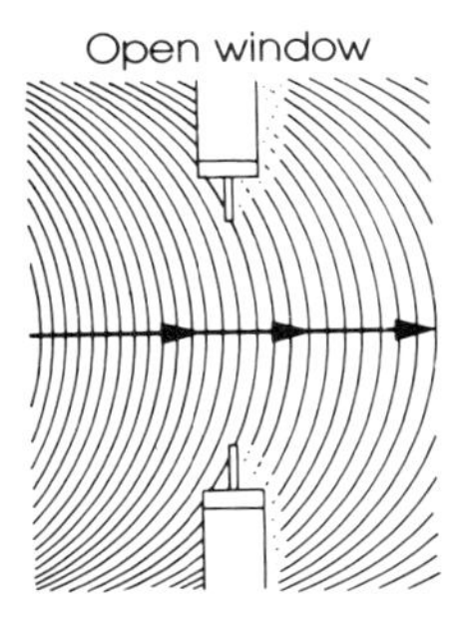


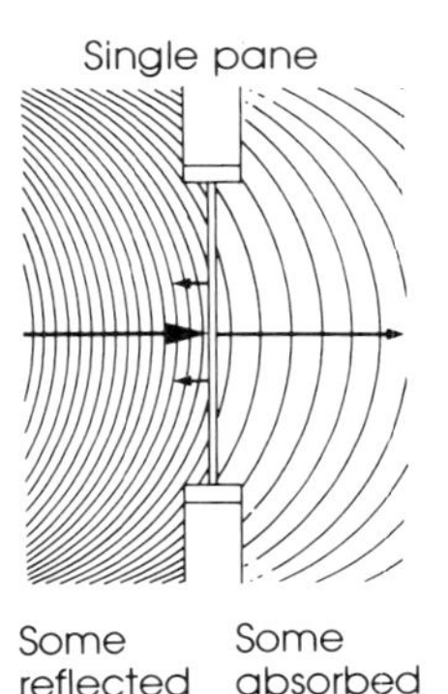


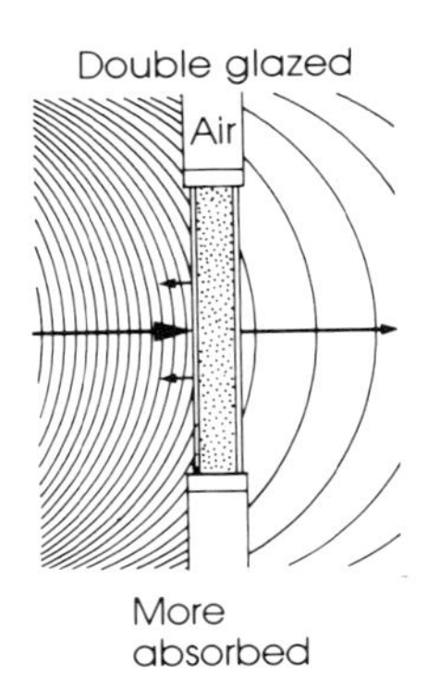


**Absorbing sound energy**

Walls

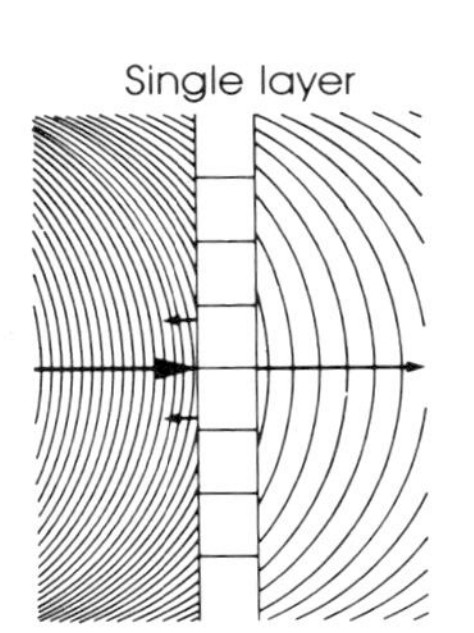


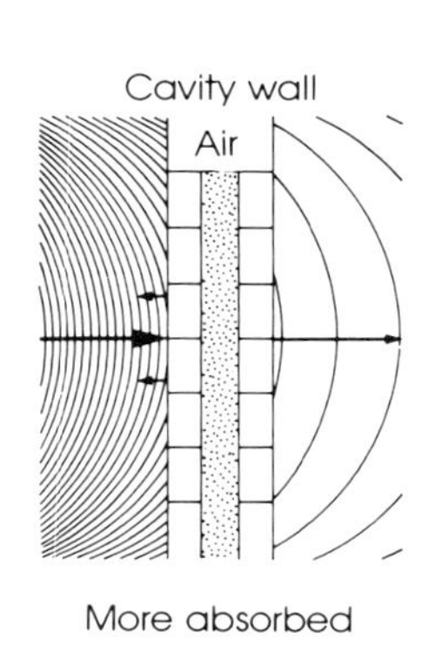


make the glass vibrate. This vibration is transmitted through the trembling glass to the air inside. But some of the 'vibration energy' is lost, as shown in the diagram above. This is how sound is absorbed.

When windows are double glazed, the vibrations have to be passed from one sheet of glass, through an air gap, to another sheet of glass to the air inside. As each layer is set into vibration some sound energy is absorbed. So double glazing can help to soundproof your home. Many people who live near large airports (like Heathrow), or busy motorways, have been given grants to help them pay for double glazing. The trouble is that they're deafened when they open their windows!

Walls are more difficult to start vibrating than windows. The walls of a house, especially cavity walls, absorb more sound energy than windows.

The insides of homes, offices and factories are important in keeping the noise down. Hard solid floors, ceilings and walls reflect sounds. In some offices and large buildings every sound seems to echo around. These reflected, unwanted sounds can be absorbed by:

1) thick, fitted carpets on the floor
2) soft wall coverings such as cork tiles or even padding
3) lowered 'false' ceilings or ceiling tiles
4) heavy curtains, padded furniture, human beings even.

The science of sounds, noises and hearing is called *acoustics.*

**ACTIVITY 18**

## How soundproof are different materials?

You can use this apparatus to compare (roughly) the soundproofing of different materials.

Apparatus for Activity 18

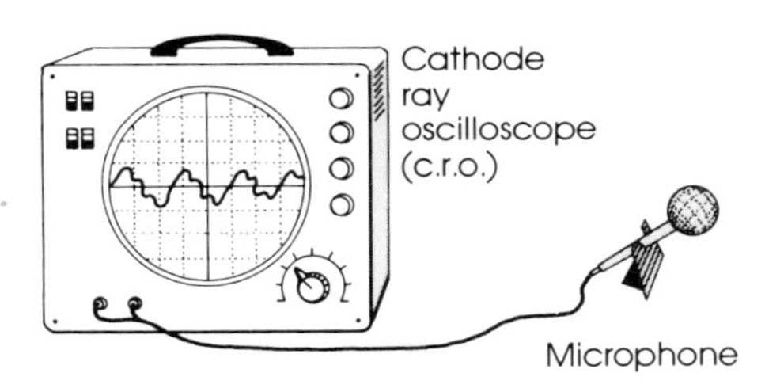


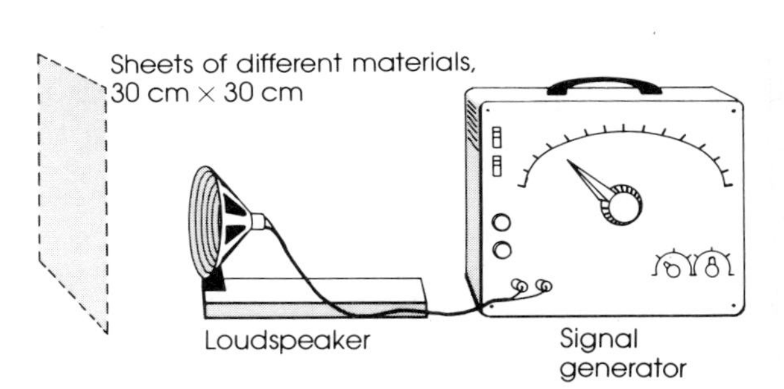


Different materials (for example, glass, cardboard, wood, polystyrene and plastic) are placed between the loudspeaker and the microphone. Look at the wave on the cathode ray oscilloscope screen with each one in place. What does the height of the wave tell you? What is the height of the wave with nothing in between?

If possible try it with two sheets of glass. (*Note.* Avoid echoes from the walls, you, and the ceiling.) Try covering the loudspeaker with a cloth. What happens? Then cover the microphone.

What does this experiment tell you about reducing noise pollution?

## DANGEROUS SOUNDS YOU CANNOT HEAR

People with good hearing can detect sound with frequencies from 15 Hz right up to 20 000 Hz (see p. 21). But unheard sounds pitched *below* these limits can be lethal. Sounds with frequencies of about 10 Hz can make people sick, dizzy and totally incapable of doing simple tasks. They are called *infrasounds*. A frequency of exactly 7 Hz can even make the organs in the human body vibrate, leading to a slow and painful death.

Sounds *above* our hearing limits can be just as dangerous — these are *ultrasounds*. Some can pierce your eardrums. Others can cause terrible pain and even madness. According to some spy films they can even be used to make your enemies confess secrets!

## QUESTIONS ON CHAPTER 5

**1** Supply words to fill in the blanks in this passage. Do not write on this page.

Sounds that are unpleasant or unwanted are called ____. The nuisance caused by unwanted sounds is called 'noise ____'. The loudness of noise is measured in ____. Noise inside homes can be reduced by ____ ____ the windows. Walls which have a ____ are good at absorbing sound energy. The study of sounds, noises and hearing is called ____. Sounds you cannot hear are called ____ (very low frequency) and ____ (very high frequency).

**2** Read carefully through this newspaper cutting then try to answer these questions:

(a) What does the word 'supersonic' mean?

(b) Does Concorde make much more noise than other planes taking off?

(c) Do you think Concorde should be allowed to fly? Make a list of its *advantages* and compare them with its *disadvantages*.

(d) What does the newspaper mean by Concorde's 'giant footprint'?

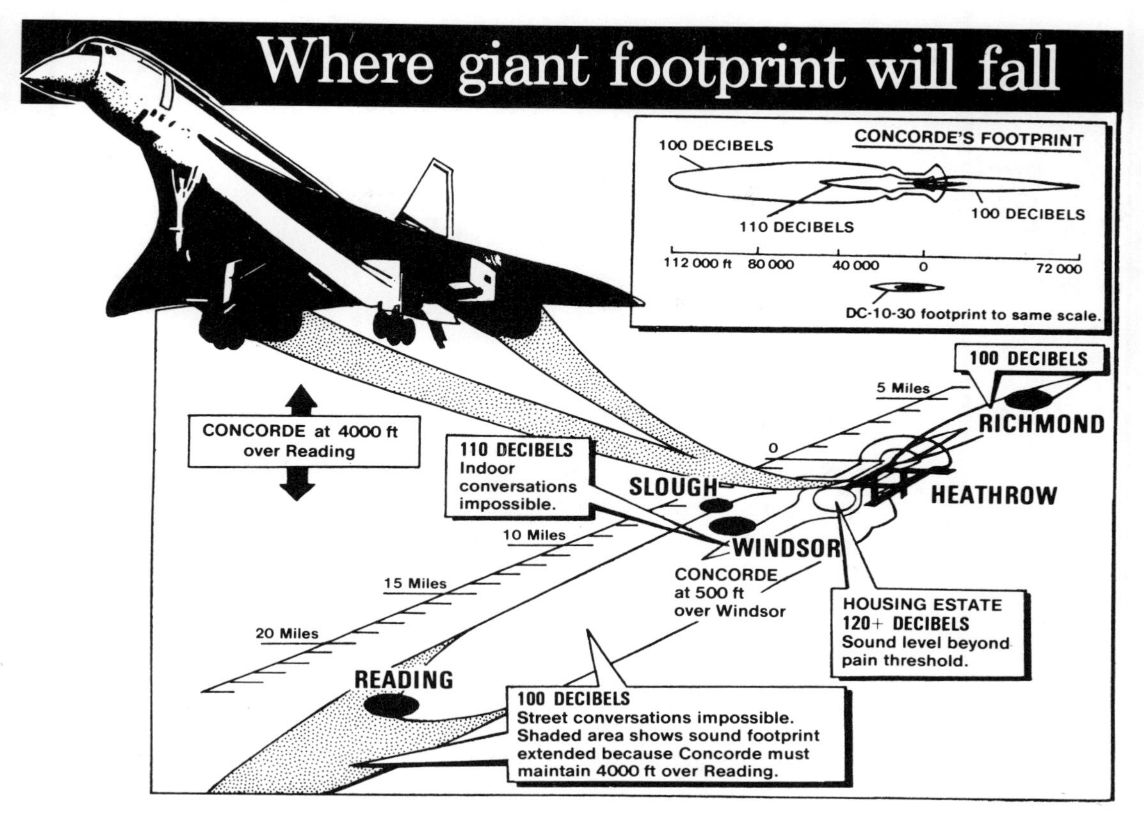


Extract from **The Observer,** 22 August 1973

# A Tube train in the sky

**by IAN MATHER**

WHEN the age of supersonic air passenger transport arrives in Britain next week with the first commercial Concorde flight to Bahrain, many people are in for a noisy shock.

Concorde's noise 'footprint' is so huge by comparison with the 'footprints' of other aircraft that people who have never had to concern themselves with over-flying aircraft will have to shout to be heard out of doors.

The 'footprint,' based on information derived from the manufacturer's own tests at Casablanca, reveals that Concorde's take-off route over the Thames Valley will make the inhabitants of Reading think they are in a noisy Tube train, while Windsor people will not even be able to hear themselves speak indoors.

This was why at the Washington hearing, last week the Bishop of Kingston, the Rt Rev. Hugh Montefiore, was prepared to bring down on his head the fury of Concorde supporters, by describing the noise from Concorde as 'a secular form of purgatory.'

The huge size of Concorde's 'footprint,' 41 times that of the DC10, which carries far more passengers, explains why the noise issue has emerged as the overriding question in Washington where the fate of Concorde is now being decided.

Neither the British Government nor the British Aircraft Corporation want to see the 'footprint' published. The Department of Industry say they have done a number of 'footprints' but have 'never seen fit to release them to the Press.' A spokesman for BAC said they considered the 'footprint' an over-estimate to the tune of 25 per cent but could provide no data to contradict it.

# THE SOUNDS OF MUSIC

## WHY ARE SOME SOUNDS MUSICAL?

Some sounds are just noises, for example, bangs, screeches, squeals, clunks and clicks. Even if you tried to put these sounds together into some sort of pattern they would still be just a noise. But other sounds, for some reason, are *musical.* Why?

The sounds of music are usually made by an instrument, such as an organ, a violin, a piano, a flute, a trumpet, a clarinet, and so on. Each one has its own particular sound. Even if they all play the same note, you can tell one from another. Each instrument has its own *quality* of sound.

But one note after another from a musical instrument does not make music. The notes have to be arranged into some sort of pattern which *sounds musical* to a listener. This depends partly on the listener himself. Music to my ears may not be music to yours. Famous composers, from Beethoven to the Beatles, seem to have the knack of arranging sounds to make music.

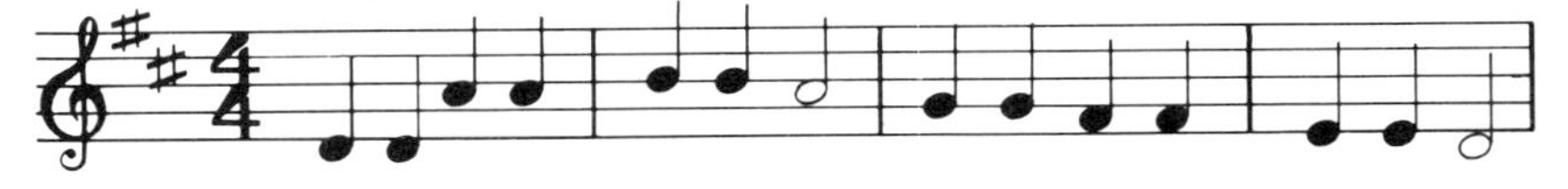

Can you work out this tune?

## DIFFERENT MUSICAL INSTRUMENTS

The sounds of music, like all other sounds, are made where something vibrates. These vibrations can be made by sucking, blowing, banging, striking or plucking.

With percussion instruments you have to bang or strike something. Triangles, bells, drums, gongs, cymbals and castanets are examples. Try to work out what is vibrating in each one of these.

Some wind instruments are made of wood (woodwind), some are made of brass. They both make sounds when air vibrates inside a tube or pipe. Some instruments you blow

How musical sounds are made

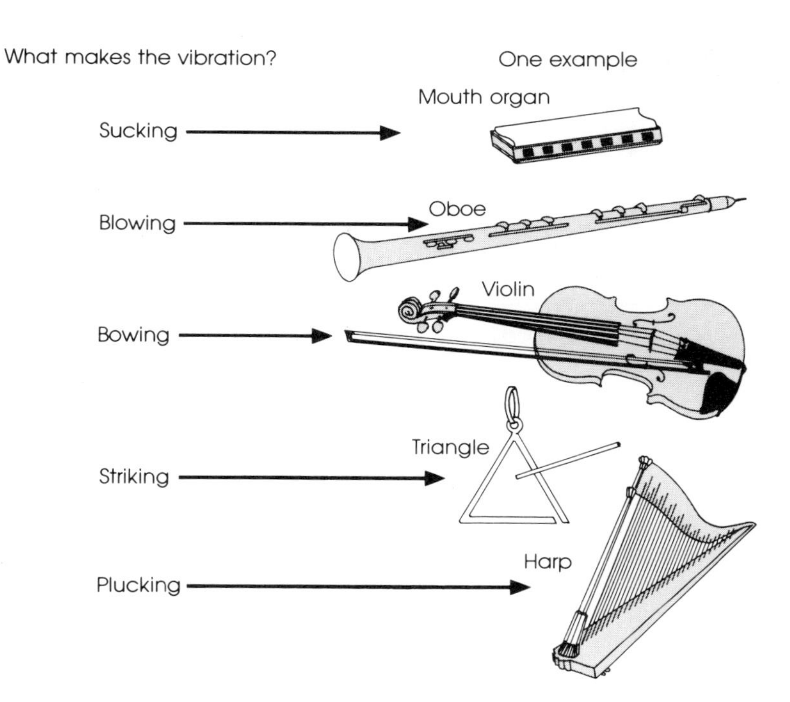


*into* through your lips, for example, a trumpet. In some instruments, like a flute or recorder, you blow *across* a sharp edge. This starts the air in the pipe vibrating.

Other wind instruments use a small *reed* which vibrates when you blow against it. This is fixed in the mouthpiece of the instrument. An oboe and a clarinet are both reed instruments.

Musical instruments come in many shapes and sizes

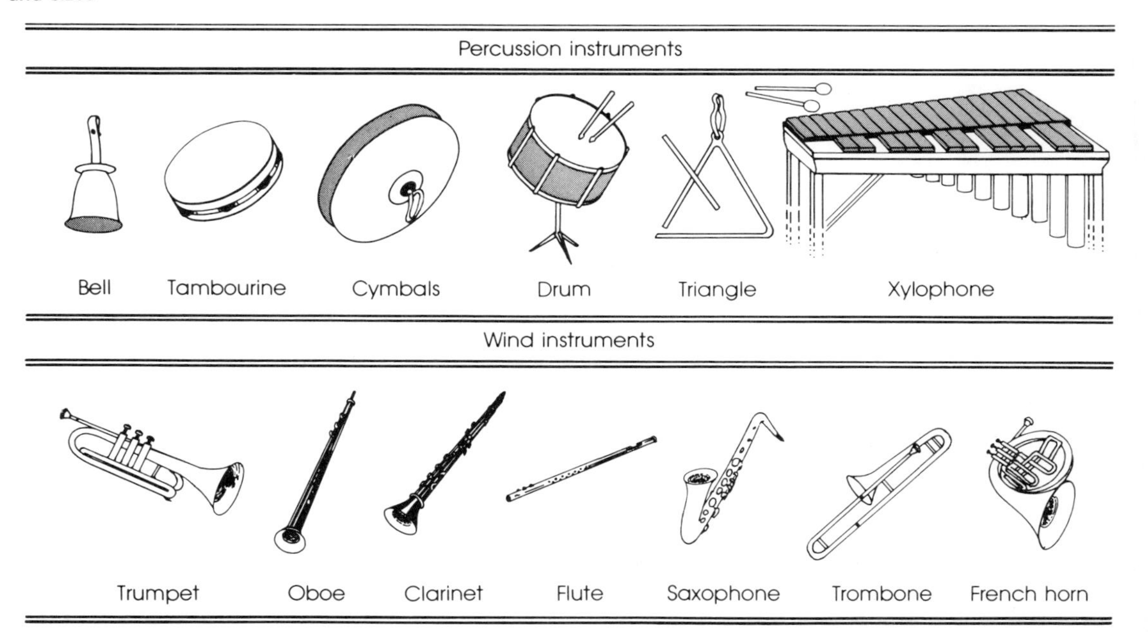

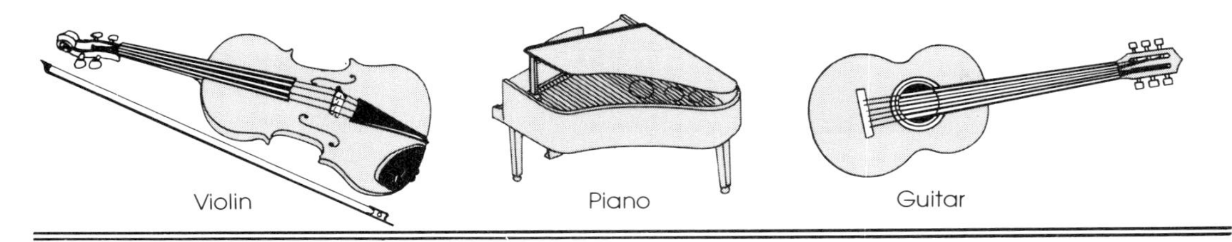


Stringed instruments use strings that vibrate, either when they are plucked or when they are stroked with a bow, for example, on a violin or a cello. On most stringed instruments (except a harp) the strings are stretched over a board or a hollow base. This is called a sounding board or a 'sound box'. The box helps to make the sound louder and longer.

A piano uses vibrating strings. But these are neither plucked nor bowed. They vibrate when a tiny hammer strikes them. In a way, the piano is a stringed, percussion instrument.

## PITCH AND FREQUENCY

The table below tells you the pitch or frequency of certain musical instruments and how they compare with other sounds.

| | *Frequency* | *Example* |
|---|---|---|
| High pitch ↑ | 50 000 Hz | Bat's squeak |
| | 20 000 Hz | Dog whistle |
| | 10 000 Hz | Ordinary whistle |
| | 2 600 Hz | Top note of a violin |
| | 1 800 Hz | Top note of a clarinet |
| | 1 000 Hz | Soprano opera singer |
| | 80 Hz | Deep bass voice |
| Low pitch ↓ | 50 Hz | Drum |

## DIFFERENT NOTES, DIFFERENT FREQUENCIES

Musical instruments can be used to produce different musical notes. Each note has a different frequency. With a stringed instrument the frequency of the note you make depends on three things:

1) how long the string is — its *length*
2) how tight the string is — its *tension*
3) how thick the string is — its *thickness*.

Shorter strings give higher notes. Longer strings give lower notes. A person playing a guitar or violin can change the length of the string which is vibrating. He does this by holding the string at different places along its length. Guitars and violins have only a few strings. But a harp has a different length string for every note, so does a piano.

The tension of each guitar or violin string can be changed. Every string is fixed to a peg, called a *tuning peg.* As you turn the peg you make the string tighter or looser. The tighter the string, the higher the note. The slacker the string, the lower the note.

Many stringed instruments have strings of different *thickness.* The violin, guitar, cello and double bass are a few examples. Thicker strings give lower notes — thinner strings give higher ones. By using different lengths, thicknesses and tensions, an instrument with only four strings (like a violin) can be made to give a wide range of musical notes.

Wind instruments use air vibrating inside a tube or pipe. The musical note depends mainly on the *length* of the pipe. The longer the pipe, the higher the frequency. With most woodwind and brass instruments you change the note by opening or closing holes along the pipe with your fingers. When all the holes are closed you are making the *longest* column of air vibrate. This makes the *lowest* note (on a recorder for example). With a trombone you change the length by moving a brass slide in and out. With the slide pushed right out you make the lowest note.

Don't forget the organ — the church organ, the mouth organ, and so on. These are wind instruments. Many pipes of different lengths (and different types) are used to make a wide range of musical notes.

## MUSICAL SCALES AND OCTAVES

Different musical notes have different frequencies. These frequencies can be arranged in *order,* to make a *musical* scale. You may have had to sing:

*doh re mi fa soh la te doh*

This is a musical scale. The *doh* at the bottom would be a lower note than the *doh* at the top. There is exactly one *octave* between them. But what is an octave?

If the scale above is played correctly (for example, on a properly tuned piano) then the second *doh* has exactly *twice* the frequency of the first. For example, if the lower *doh* is

300 Hz then the higher *doh* is 600 Hz. The two notes are one octave apart. As you go up an octave the frequency doubles.

The diagram below shows part of a piano keyboard. Each key gives a musical note with a different frequency. Each note is given a different letter, from A to G. On the piano keyboard middle C is tuned to have a frequency of 262 Hz. The other C to the left of it has a frequency of 131 Hz — exactly half. It is one octave below middle C. The note labelled C on the right is one octave above middle C. It is often called top C. This piano keyboard is tuned to 'musical pitch'. Some pianos are tuned to 'scientific pitch'. This means that middle C has a frequency of 256 Hz.

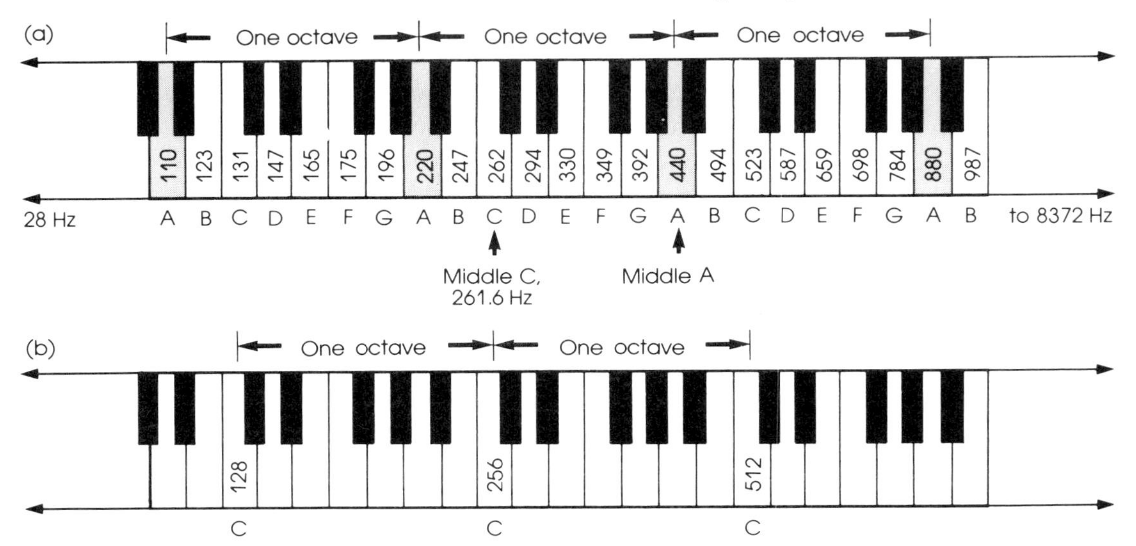


(a) Part of a piano keyboard tuned to musical pitch. (b) The same keyboard tuned to scientific pitch

## DISPLAYING MUSICAL NOTES

You have seen that musical instruments can produce notes of different frequency, or different pitch. But why does a note of the *same* pitch sound different on two different instruments? Middle C on a guitar sounds different from a middle C played on an oboe. Why?

The reason is that notes played on different instruments have a different *quality*. You can see the quality of different

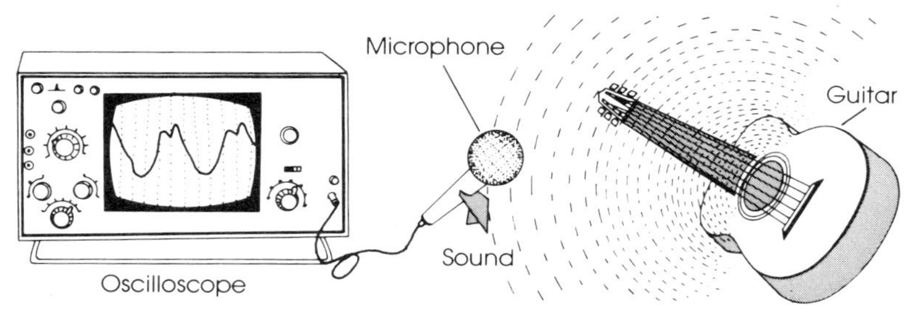


How a sound can be displayed

notes by displaying them on a screen. This is done by using an instrument called a *cathode ray oscilloscope* which has a screen like a television screen. The instrument being used is played in front of a microphone. This microphone sends electrical messages to the oscilloscope which then make a certain pattern on the screen.

Notes from different instruments make different patterns on the screen. These patterns show the *quality* of different notes. You can see that the sound from a tuning fork makes a smooth, even pattern. This note is made up of *one frequency only.* It is a pure note. But the pattern from an oboe, for example, is rough and uneven. This note is made up of a mixture of different frequencies. These extra frequencies, added to the main frequency, give musical notes their own special quality. Music played on tuning forks, which give a 'pure' note, would be quite boring. The different qualities of musical notes from different instruments make music more interesting and more enjoyable.

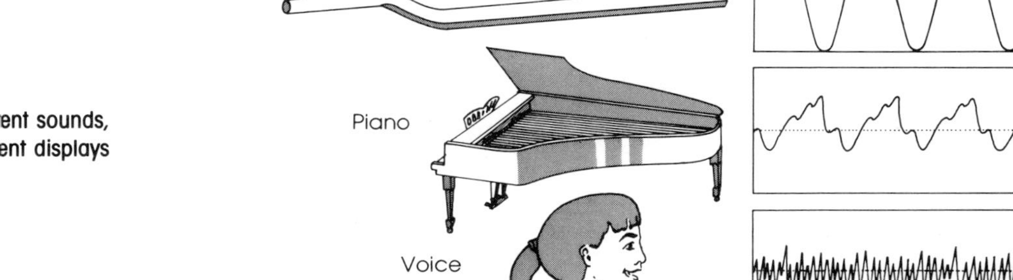


Different sounds, different displays

**ACTIVITY 19**

## Making a milk-bottle organ

You need eight empty bottles or jars of the same size. Arrange them in a row. Tap the first bottle and listen to the note. Now add a small amount of water to the second. Tap this one and listen to the note. Add slightly more water to the third bottle, more again to the fourth and so on.

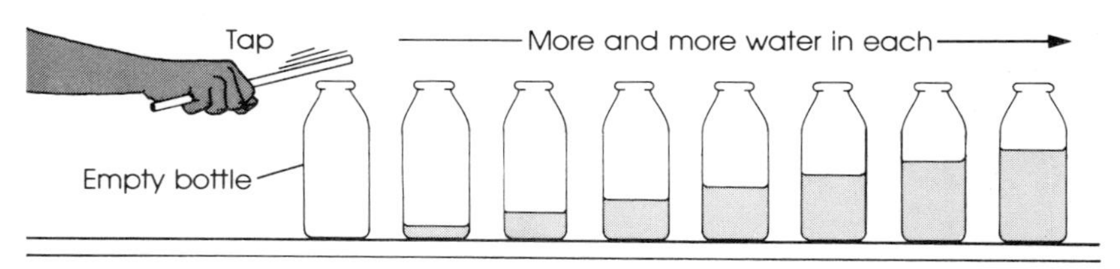


The milk-bottle organ

What do you notice about the notes from each bottle? Which bottle gives the highest note? Tap them one after the other to make a musical scale. Then try to play a simple tune, for example, 'Three Blind Mice'.

## QUESTIONS ON CHAPTER 6

**1** Do not write on this page.
Make a table like the one below to show as many examples as you can of wind, percussion, and stringed instruments.

| *Wind* | *Percussion* | *String* |
|---|---|---|
| Trumpet | Triangle | Violin |
| ———— | ———— | ———— |
| ———— | ———— | ———— |

Put each of these instruments into one of the three columns: cello, double bass, saxophone, clarinet, church organ, castanets, piano, xylophone, guitar, drum. What is actually *vibrating* in each of these instruments?

**2** Write down the name of one instrument in each case which is (a)struck (b) plucked (c) blown (d) bowed (e) sucked. In each example write down what is vibrating.

**3** With a stringed instrument write down *three* things which affect the pitch of the note you hear. How are these three things controlled by a guitar player?

**4** How can you change the *loudness* of a sound from (a) a guitar (b) a violin (c) a drum (d) a trumpet? Explain *why* the loudness changes in each example.

**5** Suppose a musical note has a frequency of 300 Hz. What is the frequency of a note (a) an octave lower (b) an octave higher? What frequency is middle A on a piano? What is the note one octave above it and one octave below?

**6** Here is a musical scale:

| *doh* | *ray* | *me* | *fah* | *soh* | *lah* | *te* | *doh* |
|---|---|---|---|---|---|---|---|
| 256 | 288 | 320 | 341.3 | 384 | 426.6 | 480 | 512 Hz |
| C | D | E | F | G | A | B | C |

What are the two notes labelled C called? What is the gap, or interval, between them? What does each of the numbers tell you? Count the number of notes in the scale. Can you see where the word 'octave' comes from?

CHAPTER

7

# 'SEEING' WITH SOUNDS

## WHY USE SOUNDS TO 'SEE'?

Most people can see. You can see this page because light rays bounce off it and reach your eyes. But no one can see through metal or to the bottom of an ocean. No one can see in the dark. No one can see through human skin. But sound waves can travel through metal, wood, brick, rock, water and skin. This is why sounds can often be useful for 'seeing' things.

This chapter explains how sounds can be used in looking for objects, measuring distances, and even finding tiny cracks in metal.

## BLIND PEOPLE USING ECHOES

Blind people cannot use light rays to see things or to find their way around. They have to use sounds to 'see' things. Whenever *you* see something your eyes are collecting the light rays coming from it. A blind person must learn to 'see' by making sense of the sound waves which are reflected from things. These reflected sounds are called *echoes.* Blind people learn to use natural echoes and sounds to find their way around.

A blind person can avoid a lamppost by listening for echoes. Most blind people can walk up to a bus shelter without walking into it. In both cases they use natural echoes. The sounds reflected may come from the scraping of their shoes, or even tapping a stick on the pavement. Some blind people may click their fingers to help them locate objects or turn a corner at the right moment.

Electronic devices are now being made which send out high-frequency sounds. A blind person can hold one in his hand and use a detector to collect the echoes. Some of these are small enough to be worn on spectacles. But only a very few people use these. Most still rely on natural echoes from natural sounds.

**ACTIVITY 20**

## 'Seeing' with echoes

Find a quiet room with a hard, solid wall. Ask someone to blindfold you. Make sure you cannot see. Stand back from the wall and walk slowly towards it, with your hands by your sides. Try to get as *close* to the wall as you can without bumping into it. How well did you do?

Now try again, this time shuffling your feet to make sounds which might echo. Try a third time, clicking your fingers as you walk. Do the echoes help you to get closer to the wall without bumping into it? Can you think of any other ways to help you find your way without eyesight?

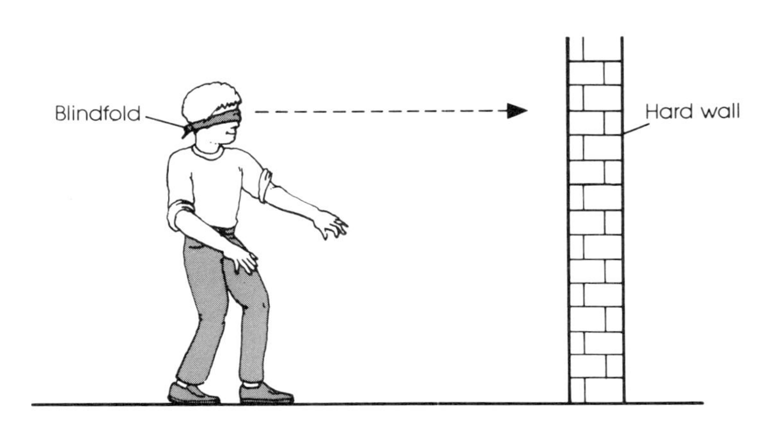


Steady!

# ECHO SOUNDING

Underwater echoes are now widely used by boats, ships and submarines. They can measure the depth of the sea below, locate shipwrecks and even detect underwater obstacles or enemies.

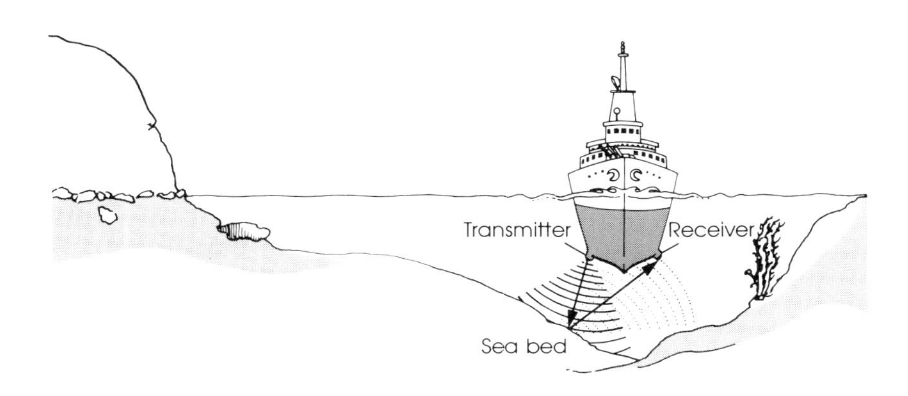


Echo sounding

Ships find the depth of sea below them by echo sounding. A special transmitter, or transducer, sends out a narrow beam of sound waves from the bottom of the ship. These are reflected off the sea bed and picked up by a receiver on the ship. The time taken for the sound to travel from the ship to the sea bed and back again is measured. The longer the sound takes, the deeper the sea. If you know the speed of sound in water, you can calculate the depth of the sea.

Modern echo sounding equipment is quite small and powerful, so many small yachts and fishing boats can carry it. Many fishermen use sound waves to look for fish — a shoal of fish makes quite a strong echo.

The use of underwater echoes to look for objects is called sonar (sound navigation and ranging). Sonar always uses very, very high-frequency sounds, as the next section explains.

## ULTRASONICS

You already know that most people can hear very high-pitched sounds, up to frequencies as high as 18 000 Hz. But many important sounds have frequencies well above this. These are called *ultrasound.* Their frequency ranges upwards from 20 000 Hz.

These high-frequency sounds are used for sonar. They can make very clear and definite echoes, especially if the sound is sent out as a narrow beam. A ship on the surface can use sonar to detect a submarine underwater. An ultrasonic beam is sent out in different directions until an echo is picked up. This tells you roughly *where* the submarine is. The time between sending the beam out and receiving it back is used to find exactly *how far away* the submarine is.

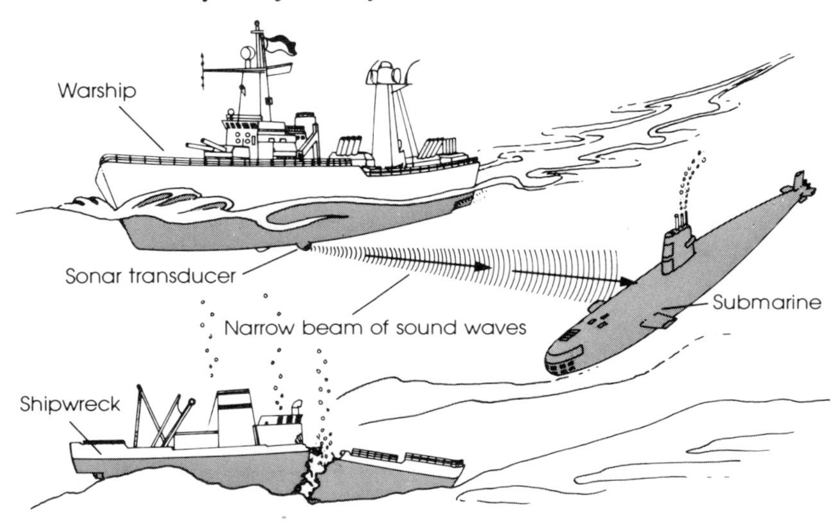


Detecting submarines or shipwrecks

Sonar equipment is used in the same way to find shipwrecks. It is also used to locate underwater oil pipes or telephone cables that need repairing. Maps of the sea bed are drawn using ultrasonic echo sounding.

People can see with ultrasound in many different ways so long as they have the right equipment for *sending out* an ultrasonic beam, and for *receiving it* back again. But some animals are actually born with this equipment. They can send out, and *hear,* ultrasonics with frequencies as high as 170 000 Hz.

## ANIMAL ULTRASONICS

Bats use ultrasonics to hunt for insects at night. They send out an ultrasonic beam which bounces back off the insect. This echo tells the bat exactly where the insect is. Bats use echoes in the same way to 'see' where they are going. Echoes reflected from anything near their flight path are picked up by the bat's quite large ears. A bat's brain is highly developed. It makes sense of these various echoes. Bats rarely make mistakes. Indeed, a bat's ability to use and interpret echoes is far more advanced than any man-made ultrasonic or radar equipment.

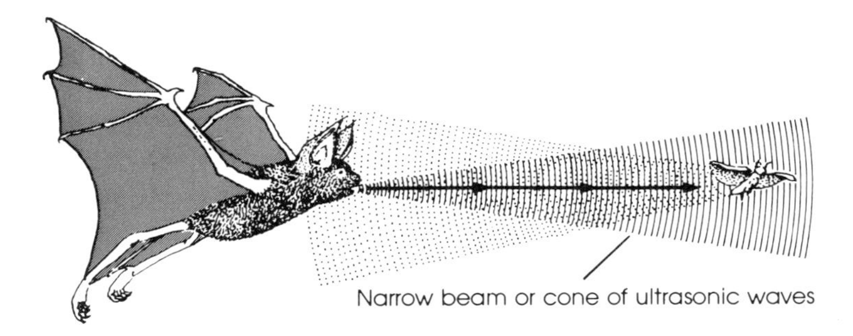


A bat uses ultrasonics

Most bats use ultrasonics well above the limit of your hearing — anything from 40 000 Hz up to 100 000 Hz. But some bats use ultrasound which you can occasionally hear — sounds below 20 000 Hz. Some of the insects that bats eat can actually hear most of a bat's ultrasound. Moths can hear sounds as high as 80 000 Hz and this certainly helps them to survive!

Dolphins and porpoises use underwater echoes for hunting and navigation. You may have seen pictures on TV of a blindfolded dolphin finding objects using its ultrasound. Like bats, their ability to use and make sense of echoes is very highly developed. They can even decide the shape, size and speed of objects using echoes. This is quite useful in hunting the right fish to eat! Whales, porpoises and dolphins also use ultrasonics to communicate with each other.

## USING ULTRASONICS

Different types of tissue inside the human body send back different types of echo from an ultrasonic beam. This fact can be used to 'see' inside a human body. A beam of ultrasonic waves is sent into a patient's body. The reflected waves are picked up and can be displayed on a screen. This is called *ultrasonic scanning.* Scanning can be used to 'see' the exact position of an unborn baby inside its mother's womb. It can be used to search for tumours and other abnormalities in the abdomen, and for studying the heart.

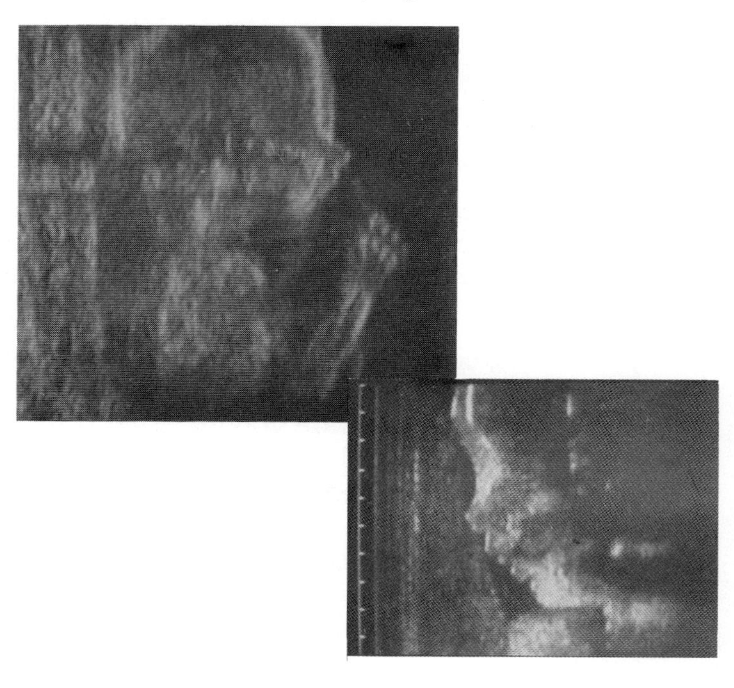

An ultrasonic scan of an unborn baby

Ultrasonics can clean dental and medical equipment. A beam of ultrasound 'shakes off' the dirt.

An ultrasonic beam with very high energy can also be used to cut human tissue. This is one of the ways that it can be used in surgery.

In industry, ultrasound is used for cleaning. Large metal objects such as the parts of an engine can have the dirt shaken off them by ultrasonic waves. There is another important use for ultrasonics in industry — an ultrasonic beam can detect tiny cracks in metal, concrete or rubber. A tiny crack will send back its own echo. The exact position of the crack can be found. British Rail has its own 'ultrasonic rail testing train'. This can find hidden cracks inside the metal railway lines. Ultrasonic scanners slide along the rails sending waves into the metal. Unusual or unexpected echoes are signs of a hidden crack.

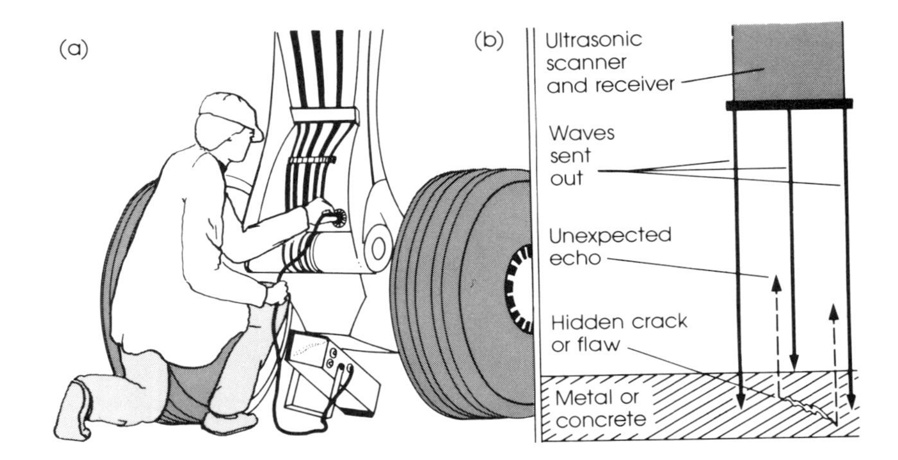


(a) Looking for cracks in an aeroplane undercarriage.
(b) The echo from a crack

Ultrasonic waves can be used for *mixing.* Liquids which don't normally mix, like oil and water, can be shaken together by ultrasound. This can be useful in food factories for preparing all kinds of food stuffs.

Geologists use ultrasonics to explore the earth beneath their feet. A beam of ultrasound is sent down into the earth. Some rocks are good *reflectors* of ultrasonic waves and will send back a strong echo. Other rocks are good *absorbers* and these make deeper echoes weaker. By studying the echoes which come back, geologists can tell what rocks and minerals lie under the surface. The main use of ultrasonics in exploration is hunting for oil. Geologists can often tell whether oil lies beneath the surface by studying ultrasonic echoes.

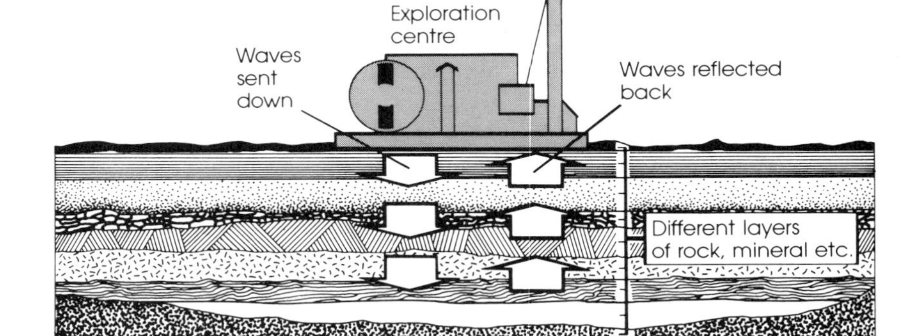


Exploring the Earth's crust with ultrasonics

## QUESTIONS ON CHAPTER 7

**1** Supply words to fill in the blanks in the following passage. Do not write on this page.
Light waves can travel through air and empty ____. But sound waves can travel through brick, ____ and ____. This is why they are often useful. Blind people can find their way around by using natural ____. Ships can find the depth of water below them using ____ sounding. The use of underwater ____ is called sonar. This stands for ____ ____ ____ ____. Sonar uses very high-frequency sounds called ____. Their frequency is always above ____ Hz. Three animals which use their own sonar are ____, ____, and ____,

**2** Explain why sound waves are often more useful for 'seeing' things than light rays.

**3** Describe how a ship can use sound waves to (a) search for shipwrecks, (b) spot an enemy submarine, and (c) find the depth of the sea below it.

**4** Read this passage carefully then try to answer the questions that follow it:

STRANDING

Hundreds of whales and dolphins die on beaches every year because of 'stranding'. Huge whales become stranded in shallow water on a sandy beach and find that they cannot get back into deep water. For some reason other whales come to join them, perhaps to try and help. Eventually there may be twenty or thirty whales stranded on the beach. They struggle to escape but few succeed, even with human help. The whales die a slow and unpleasant death.

Stranding in large numbers is peculiar to whales and dolphins. Nobody knows quite why it happens but three reasons have been suggested:

1) One whale gets into trouble and comes aground on the beach. It sends ultrasonic signals to other whales, for help. Eventually more and more whales become stranded.
2) For some unknown reason the sonar of whales and dolphins may go wrong. They receive strange echoes from the beach or cliffs which they interpret wrongly.
3) Stranding may be a form of 'mass suicide'. (This explanation seems the least likely.)

(a) Explain what each of these words from the passage means: *stranding, sonar, interpret.*

(b) Explain what this sentence means: 'Stranding is peculiar to whales and dolphins'. Why do you think this is?

(c) Which explanation for stranding do you think is the *most* likely? Explain your reasons.

## CROSSWORD 1

First, trace this grid on to a piece of paper (or photocopy this page). Then fill in the answers. Do not write on this page.

### Across

1, 8 down They measured the velocity of sound in water (5, 8)
2 Sounds we all enjoy (5)
5 All sounds are produced by ____ (10)
9 A ____ sound is produced by strong 5 across (4)
10 A bone in your middle ear (6)
11 Sound would take about ____ seconds to travel 1000 metres in air (5)
12 Another bone in your middle ear (5)
13 The doctor may listen to them with a stethoscope (5)
14 Sounds we don't enjoy (6)

### Down

1 A third bone in your middle ear (7)
3 It can break the sound barrier (8)
4 The higher the frequency of a sound, the higher the ____ (5)
6 The study of sounds in buildings (9)
7 It may send a pulse to the sea bed (9)
8 See 1 across (8)
11 When you ____ you are making sounds (4)

## CROSSWORD 2

First, trace this grid on to a piece of paper (or photocopy this page). Then fill in the answers. Do not write on this page.

### Across

4 When you ____ a pipe hole you change the note (4)
6 Animal that uses ultrasonic echoes (7)
7 A sound at 7 Hz can even be ____ (5)
8 A returning sound (4)
10 A device for channelling the human voice (9)
12 Ultrasonic flier (3)
14, 15 down We use them to produce sounds (5, 6)
15 See 13 down (5)
16 If 'doh' is 256 Hz, ____ is 480 Hz (3)
17 A nearby falling leaf has a loudness of about ____ decibels (3)
19 What a racket! (3)
20 It may vibrate to produce a musical note (4)
21 The loudness from a ____ can be as high as 85 decibels (3)
22 A percussion instrument (4)
23 A ____ sound is produced by weak vibrations (4)
24 Connell founded the Noise Abatement ____ (7)

### Down

1 A type of singer with a fairly high voice (4)
2 These animals also use ultrasonic echoes (6)
3 We cannot hear them but they are dangerous (11)
5 Musical instrument (5)
6 Unit of loudness (7)
9 Your ears convert sound waves into ____ impulses (5)
11 ____ aids use a microphone to pick up sound waves (7)
13 The ____ of a 15 across 1 m away has a loudness of 20–30 decibels (4)
15 See 14 across (6)
16 A public address system (6)
17 Wind instruments use air vibrating inside pipes or ____ (5)
18 Personal hi-fi can make you partially ____ (4)